Twayne's English Authors Series

Sylvia E. Bowman, *Editor*

INDIANA UNIVERSITY

James Elroy Flecker

TEAS 185

James Elroy Flecker

JAMES ELROY FLECKER

By JOHN M. MUNRO
American University of Beirut

TWAYNE PUBLISHERS
A Division of G. K. Hall & Co.
Boston, Massachusetts, U. S. A.

1976

Library of Congress Cataloging in Publication Data

Munro, John Murchison.
  James Elroy Flecker.

  (Twayne's English authors series ; TEAS 185)
  Bibliography: p. 135 - 38.
  Includes index.
  1. Flecker, James Elroy, 1881-1915.   I. Title.
PR6011.L4Z73   821'.9'12   75-46531
ISBN 0-8057-6656-1

MANUFACTURED IN THE UNITED STATES OF AMERICA

67022

For
KAREN, PETER, STEPHEN, and KIRSTEN
to whom the Brumana pines whisper
a different story

Contents

About the Author

John M. Munro received his B. A. (Honors) from Durham University in 1955, and his Ph. D. from Washington University, St. Louis, in 1961. Professor Munro has taught at the universities of North Carolina, Toronto, and London, England, and since 1965 has been at the American University of Beirut, Lebanon, where he is now professor of English.

A specialist in late nineteenth- and twentieth-century literature, Professor Munro is author or co-author of *The Worlds of Fiction* (1964); *English Poetry in Transition* (1968); *Images and Memories* (1970); *A Poet and His Country* (1970); *The Decadent Poetry of the Eighteen Nineties* (1970); *The Royal Aquarium: Failure of a Victorian Compromise* (1971); *Selected Poems of Theo Marzials* (1973); and *Arthur Symons* (Twayne's English Authors Series, 1969).

Preface

John Heath-Stubbs, the author of a bleak, prophetic poem about the future of poetry, chose James Elroy Flecker as an example to support his view that generations to come would have little time for those who sought to "conquer" by writing verse; for who, indeed, "reads Elroy Flecker now?"

"TO A POET A THOUSAND YEARS HENCE"

I who am dead a thousand years
And wrote this crabbed post-classic screed
Transmit it to you — though with doubts
That you possess the skill to read,

Who, with your pink mutated eyes,
Crouched in the radioactive swamp,
Beneath a leaking shelter, scan
These lines beside a flickering lamp;

Or in some plastic paradise
Of pointless gadgets, if you dwell,
And finding all your wants supplied
Do not suspect it may be Hell.

But does our art of words survive —
Do bards within that swamp rehearse
Tales of the twentieth century,
Nostalgic, in rude epic verse?

Or do computers churn it out —
In lieu of songs of War and Love,
Neat slogans by the State endorsed
And prayers to them, who sit above?

How shall we conquer — all our pride
Fades like a summer sunset's glow:
Who will read me when I am gone —
For who reads Elroy Flecker now?

Unless, dear poet, you were born,
Like me, a deal behind your time,
There is no reason you should read,
And much less understand, this rhyme.[1]

In his day, however, Flecker was regarded by Edmund Gosse, arbiter
of literary taste in England during the first two decades of the twentieth century; by W. B. Yeats; by Gilbert Murray, the great Classics
scholar; and by some editors as by "far the greatest poet . . . barring
Yeats."[2] Today, it is difficult to see why Flecker should claim greater
attention than other of his now half-forgotten contemporaries:
Lascelles Abercrombie, John Drinkwater, J. C. Squire, and all the
other minor poets who contributed to the so-called "Georgian"
anthologies.

Certainly, Flecker's lyrical, fin-de-siècle reveries and his Romantic
enthusiasm for the fairy-tale exoticism of the mysterious East appear
even less relevant to our era than does the poetry of Rupert Brooke,
Flecker's friend and contemporary, who also sang of the parklike
prettiness of the English countryside and who regarded life (and
death) through a Cotswolds haze. Brooke's promising career, cut
short by death—if not on the battlefield, at least close to it—lent a
tragic dimension to his writings; and, though his verses now seem
thinner than they once did, he lives on as a symbol—as an eternal
reminder of the fickleness of Fortune, who chose to cut a potentially
fruitful branch which might have grown "full straight." Flecker, by
contrast, though intellectually capable, was a comparative failure;
he was unable to achieve success in either his academic studies or in
his career as a consular official. Like Brooke's, Flecker's life was
short, but his was without glory: he died quietly in a hospital bed,
not from wounds received in combat, but from tuberculosis caused
by a chill after an ill-advised swim in the Black Sea. And such is not
the life or death from which legends are made.

But Flecker deserves to be remembered, for few poets had greater
love or respect for language than he; and the fact that his works are
now hardly ever read and that his name is almost forgotten is as
much a criticism of the prevailing standards of literary taste as of the
poet himself. Flecker was, above all, a literary craftsman; and his

poems, though mostly slight, are artfully constructed. His diction is rarely careless; his meter is almost invariably tight and controlled. He is a poet rather than a prophet — a writer who, though usually lumped together with the Georgians, is perhaps best appreciated as a late survival of the nineteenth-century European Parnassian tradition. His is not a poetry of ideas; it is an expression of the belief that good poetry finds its beauty in perfection of form and clarity of outline. That he had comparatively little to say is true, but in his respect for language and form he deserves to be regarded as a serious poet who constantly strove to achieve artistic perfection.

Flecker's prose, however, is less distinguished than his verse. His literary criticism, though generally sound, tends to be conventional rather than inspired; it reveals admiration for those formal qualities which are apparent in his own verse. His descriptive essays are slight, but they do show that he had an eye for the amusing or arresting detail; his visionary fantasies are clever, but not especially profound; and his long dialogue "The Grecians" is a readable account of an ideal, though hardly practical, educational system. His major prose work, *The King of Alsander*, a novel, is an uneven mixture of social comment, high romance, farce, and fine writing — a patchy, formless work whose uncertainty of direction all too clearly demonstrates its painful history of composition: a youthful jeu d'esprit which underwent a series of revisions over a period of years, it was forced into print a few months before Flecker's death.

On the other hand, Flecker's two poetic dramas, *Don Juan* and *Hassan*, are more noteworthy, for both reflect his scrupulous concern for form and expression. *Don Juan*, the less impressive of the two, mainly on account of its schizoid nature, is composed of almost equal portions of political propaganda and tragic romance. *Hassan*, however, published in 1922 and spectacularly produced by Basil Dean a year later, was widely acclaimed; and it must surely rank among the more successful verse dramas of the twentieth century. This work is certainly Flecker's most significant single achievement; in it he for once endeavors not simply "to conquer" through words but also to enquire into the very nature and function of art.

Flecker is also interesting in that his life provides a valuable insight into that comfortable era we call Edwardian, that decade at the beginning of the twentieth century which separates the Victorian age from the modern. Of course, to isolate this period from the years preceding and those which came after is to simplify the course of history. Nevertheless, those years from the turn of the century until the 1914 - 18 war do seem in retrospect to have had a comfortable, golden quality which sets them apart from their immediate past and future, and Flecker came to maturity during this period. Born into a moderately well-to-do, cultivated family, Flecker as a child scolded his nanny, and he later wrote rather precocious, self-important letters to his parents from the boarding school where he was sent preparatory to entering the university.

After being reared in the somewhat stifling security of a staunchly religious household, where he was taught to uphold the traditional British public-school virtues and to support Queen and country, he went to Oxford. There, as an undergraduate, he was by turns gaily irresponsible and desperately earnest, simultaneously mocking traditional values and seeking for "Truth." At the university, he studied, inevitably, Classics, and later Eastern languages. Afterwards, he entered the consular service, where from all accounts he was a far from efficient officer; he devoted the greater part of his energies to writing poems rather than to official dispatches, to picnicking, to entertaining, and to playing the English gentleman abroad. When sickness made it impossible for him to maintain even the appearance of attending to his official duties, he received a modest but by no means insignificant pension which enabled him to retire; and, thanks to the generosity of his parents, he passed the remaining months of his life in relative comfort in a Swiss sanitarium.

In a sense Flecker was fortunate to die when he did. He enjoyed the Indian summer which preceded the horrifying freeze of the 1914 - 1918 war, seemingly unaware that the end of an era was at hand. He passed away quietly while life for a man of even moderate means could be comfortable, genteel, and elegant. He never experienced real financial stress; he was never called upon to work really hard; he never harbored doubts about the supremacy of the English race, the stability of his country's economy, or the invincibility of her armed forces. Belonging to a privileged class, he lived in a complacent, comfortable world; and his career serves as a nostalgic reminder of a time and ethos which today seem as remote as the *Arabian Nights* dream world which he evoked in *Hassan* and in many of his poems.

Because we have in Flecker a reflected portrait of the Edwardian age, I have felt it necessary in the following pages to devote considerable space to biography, taking the opportunity to set the record straight concerning his supposed effectiveness as a consular officer. Other chapters deal consecutively with selected examples of Flecker's poetry, the bulk of his prose, and his two dramas. In discussing these works I have endeavored to emphasize his steady devotion to the ideals of careful, deliberate literary craftsmanship. Finally, taking my cue from John Heath-Stubbs, whose poem on Flecker suggests that, after all, to care for art is to care for life, I show that Flecker also subscribed to such a belief, one which sets him apart from other exponents of the commonly held notion of the meaning of "art for art's sake." Flecker himself asserted in his essay "The Public as Art Critic," that "dullness, weakness, bad workmanship, vulgar thought, shoddy sentiment" are ultimately "slanders on mankind."[3] Art is important, but not for itself alone: its true value lies in that its perfection is an affirmation of the glory of life itself. This awareness that art is, ultimately, for life's sake makes Flecker, an otherwise somewhat unsympathetic figure, more endearing. This awareness also justifies our considering him with more sympathy and with greater seriousness than he usually receives.

JOHN M. MUNRO

Jelsa, Hvar

Acknowledgments

I am indebted to several publishers who have granted me permission to reprint material for which they hold the copyright: to A. P. Watt and Son and William Heinemann for permission to publish extracts from Flecker's *Don Juan, Hassan,* and *Collected Prose;* to the Richards Press for permission to publish selections from Flecker's *Collected Poems;* to John Murray for allowing me to include a lengthy extract from Edward Atiyah's *An Arab Tells His Story;* to David Higham Associates and Mr. John Heath-Stubbs for permission to reprint his poem "To a Poet a Thousand Years Hence." I wish to thank also the Public Records Office, London, for allowing me permission to publish information concerning Flecker's request for a transfer to the general consular service and also parts of Consul-General Cumberbatch's official report about the Italian bombardment.

Once again it is my pleasure to record my thanks to the Arts and Sciences Research Committee at the American University of Beirut for providing generous aid in the preparation of the typescript. I am also indebted to several colleagues and friends — Bassem Ra'd, Alexander Sinclair, Adnan Haydar, and Nada Adib — all of whom contributed to this study in various ways. The British Embassy in Beirut graciously allowed me to reproduce the photograph of Flecker on the dust jacket, one made from a portrait hanging in the ambassador's office.

Finally, I wish to record a deep debt of gratitude to my friends in Beirut, especially my colleague Suheil Bushrui, whose many kindnesses have preserved me from seeing Lebanon through Flecker's eyes.

Chronology

1884 Herman James Elroy Flecker born at Gilmore Road, Lewisham, London, on November 5.
1886 Dr. William Herman Flecker, the poet's father, appointed first headmaster of Dean Close School, Cheltenham, which remained Flecker's real home for the rest of his life.
1893 Flecker enters Dean Close as a pupil.
1894 The first of many family visits to Southborne, on the south coast of England near Bournemouth, where Dr. Flecker had a small house. Flecker becomes deeply attached to the surrounding countryside; recalls it later in several of his poems written abroad.
1899 "Flakes," Flecker's first poem to appear in print, published in the September issue of *The Decanian.*
1901 Flecker enters Uppingham School; he distinguishes himself as a brilliant but erratic student.
1902 Having won an open scholarship in Classics, Flecker enters Trinity College, Oxford; gains a modest reputation as a conversationalist and esthete.
1906 Flecker deeply distressed after receiving only a third-class degree. With Jack Beazley, he published *The Best Man* for "Eights Week," soon afterwards, leaving Oxford for a position as schoolmaster at Mr. Simmons' School, Holly Hill, Hampstead, London.
1907 Flecker publishes his first volume of verse, *The Bridge of Fire.*
1908 After brief stints as a schoolmaster at Mill Hill School, London, and at Aysgarth School in the West Riding of Yorkshire, Flecker goes to Caius College, Cambridge, to study Oriental languages for the student interpretors' examinations, preparatory to entering the consular service.

1909 Flecker meets Eleanor Finlayson at a Fabian summer camp; asks her to marry him.

1910 Flecker enters the consular service; leaves England in June for Constantinople, where he had been posted as vice consul, his engagement to Eleanor Finlayson having been broken. In September, he catches a chill after bathing in the Black Sea. The doctors discover traces of tuberculosis and recommend that he return home. Enters sanitarium at Cranham in the Cotswolds; soon begins to feel better. Flecker publishes *Thirty-Six Poems* and "The Grecians." Visits Paris.

1911 In March, believing himself cured, returns to Constantinople; one month later, transferred to Smyrna; has a relapse; forced to return home again on sick leave. On May 25, marries Hellé Skiardaressi; the couple retire to Corfu for their honeymoon; Flecker begins his best known work, *Hassan*. In September, he is transferred to Beirut as vice consul. Publishes *The Scholars' Italian Book* and *Forty-Two Poems*.

1912 The Fleckers reside at Areiya, where they are visited by T. E. Lawrence. In November, Flecker in England again; tries unsuccessfully to obtain a university teaching position.

1913 Returns to Lebanon; health breaks down again; necessitates his removal from Beirut and confinement in a sanitarium at Leysin, Switzerland. Publishes his best volume of poems, *The Golden Journey to Samarkand*.

1914 In May, Flecker is removed to another Swiss sanitarium, at Davos; his health begins to deteriorate rapidly. Continues to write, however; publishes his only novel, *The King of Alsander*.

1915 Flecker dies on January 3. His last volume of poems, *The Old Ships*, published posthumously.

1916 *Collected Poems* published; contains most of his previously published verse, much of it revised since its first appearance in print.

1920 *Collected Prose* published; contains most but not all of his literary criticism, prose sketches, and translations, as well as "The Grecians" and the preface to *The Golden Journey to Samarkand*.

1922 *Hassan* published.

1923 Basil Dean's production of *Hassan* opens on September 20 at His Majesty's Theatre, London; Henry Ainley and Leon Quartermaine play the leading roles.

Chronology

1925 *Don Juan* published.
1926 The first performance of *Don Juan* at the 300 Club.
1951 First publication of the acting version of *Hassan,* as revised for the stage by Basil Dean.

CHAPTER 1

The Early Years

I *School*

HERMAN Elroy Flecker — in 1902 he dropped Herman and substituted James, the name by which he is more generally known — was born in Gilmore Road, Lewisham, London, on November 5, 1884. His father, W. H. Flecker, was a schoolmaster and an ordained clergyman of the Church of England who in 1886 was appointed headmaster of Dean Close School, Cheltenham, which remained James' real home for the rest of his life. Flecker's father appears to have been a devout, stern, but nonetheless kind man who won the respect of his students — a man whose "own very real piety and faith," it is said, "preserved him from sterility in his soul and in his work."[1] His home had a friendly, cultivated atmosphere; the family gathered for musical evenings and for intellectual and literary discussions; and the father generated an "enormous vitality" which his children affectionately remembered in later life.[2]

Although Flecker's parents seem to have had little understanding of their son's wayward personality, they tried in their own way to provide him with the warmth and security he seems so desperately to have needed. Through the nursery window young James could view a rose garden; and this image, closely associated with the emotional security of home, remained with him throughout his life.[3] As a schoolboy at Dean Close, Flecker distinguished himself in all subjects and participated in a number of extracurricular activities: he played the violin at school concerts, and he held the offices of curator of philately and curator of geology in the Field Club.[4]

At the age of thirteen, he was writing poetry, much of it imbued with religious feeling;[5] and in the September, 1899, issue of *The Decanian*, the school magazine, there appeared what must be his first published poem, "Flakes: A Sanatorium Ditty." An unexcep-

tional piece of writing, even for a child of fourteen, it serves as a
salutary reminder that, though the bulk of Flecker's poetry, early
and late, is tinged with melancholy, he did have a sense of humor
and a fondness for burlesque which never entirely deserted him. The
opening stanza reads:

> Make loud lament, ye Muses nine,
>   Oh, turn ye ashy pale,.
> Your follower the rash has got,
>   Oh, willow weep and wail.
> No more his waking eyes shall see
>   Leckhampton bathed in light,
> No more he'll wake the prefect up,
>   By snoring in the night.

And the poem concludes:

> Ah me! I'll keep my pecker up,
>   My blood shan't lose its heat,
> Nil Desperandum, while, oh while
>   There's something left to eat.
> Cheer up my soul: we've said farewell
>   To bread and milk and slops,
> Ha, carry on Hope's flag ahead,
>   I'll soon be eating chops.[6]

In 1901, Flecker left Dean Close for Uppingham School where he
became a friend of Frank Savery, with whom he kept in close touch
until his own death. About this time he began to experience religious
doubts, expressed in a long letter to his mother dated October 27,
1901; and also about this time he began to take poetic composition
seriously. He completed a long, romantic poem, "Phaon," one consciously modeled on William Morris' "Jason," which he wrote in a
small manuscript book and sent to his parents.[7] At Uppingham
Flecker's individualism and independent spirit came to the fore;
and, according to his housemaster, Mr. Haines, his schoolmates
regarded him as something of a "freak." "His effect," said Haines,
"was that of a visitor from another sphere who bursts in upon our
school-life with a challenge to its most sacred traditions. He sneered
at our moral standards, which were curiously perverse; he tolerated
our worship of games but damaged it more by his toleration than he
could have done by open revolt; he mocked our schoolboy heroes

unless they could show a truer title to respect than mere dexterity of hand and eye; he went his own way, without affectation or self-consciousness."[8]

II *Oxford*

At Uppingham, Flecker's scholastic capabilities continued to mature; but, an erratic student, he was "casual, eclectic, brilliant";[9] when he went in 1902 to Trinity College, Oxford, on an open scholarship to study Classics, signs already existed that, though his ability was unquestionable, his independent spirit and volatile temperament would deter academic success. This indication proved to be correct for, though he seems to have attained social distinction as a lively conversationalist and was generally recognized as a witty, amusing companion, he could only manage in 1906 a "third" in "Greats."

Oxford undoubtedly exerted a profound influence upon Flecker. At the time of his attendance, the influence of Walter Pater and Oscar Wilde, and of all the other young esthetes who had gathered around them, was still felt; but, with the passing of the masters, the Esthetic cult had lost both its serious spokesmen and its more extreme practitioners. For all its factitious extravagance, the Esthetic cult of the 1890s had been built on relatively solid foundations: the Esthetic philosophy of Walter Pater; the practice of the French Symbolists; and the example of the English Pre-Raphaelites. Confronted by the rigid conventionalism and by the Philistinism of the contemporary middle class, Estheticism, and its more extreme manifestation, Decadence, had hardened into passionately held convictions. Thus, though there were a vast number of poseurs in the 1890s who feigned a rapturous dedication to the cause of beauty and who self-consciously cultivated the exotic and the bizarre, hoping thereby to *épater la bourgeoisie,* originally and essentially Estheticism was a genuine if somewhat ill-defined artistic movement.[10]

By 1902, however, whatever sincerity Estheticism had had largely disappeared. At Oxford, to be sure, there were still dandies galore who, resplendent in satin waistcoats, strutted down "the High," affected the nice conduct of a cane, and engaged in the evenings in languid colloquies about art in heavily curtained rooms, the air thick with incense; but their behavior was more of a pose than a conviction. Oxford during these years has been well described by Douglas Goldring, who was himself an undergraduate there at the time.

"Instead of the fierce and violent reactions of the 'nineties," he writes, "when those who could not bear the public school atmosphere signalised their escape from the prison-house by rushing to extremes of morbid decadence, there was a more widely diffused cultivation of the arts and less persecution of the poseur, with the result that young men became on the whole less closely wedded to their poses."

Consequently, "to be a 'decadong' was really more a rag than anything else, and I don't suppose that any of the youths who in slightly intoxicated moments recited the 'credo of the despairing decadent' would have gone to the stake for it." Therefore, although "the 'nineties were cultivated with rapture in the nineteen-hundreds, and the extravagances and eccentricities of the earlier period were reproduced with painstaking zeal," the point of view had changed — "the 'ennui' was factitious."[11] Undergraduates who wished to be in "the swim" wrote poetry; they strove to be "wondrous"; they cultivated an appearance of sensitivity (if possible, even of frailty); and they professed to be "gnawed by secret despairs." Yet their performances were conducted with good humor, and a young poet could write:

> There is no hope to be hoped for,
> There is no new word to be said:
> All ends are as shadows of shadows,
> Pale ghosts of things dead.
>
> The good and the evil, what are they?
> I am weary of ease as of strife:
> The days as they drag are made heavy
> With loathing of life, . . .

These lines, which would have been regarded fifteen years previously as inept but sincere, were probably written with the tongue firmly in cheek.[12]

This Oxford Flecker knew during the early years of the twentieth century, and soon after his arrival there he too joined the fashionable band of poseurs. He was led, as one of his contemporaries put it, "by his highly artistic sense . . . into the company of brilliant bohemians and into the by-paths of exotic literature." This influence appears in his first published volume of poems, *The Bridge of Fire*, which appeared in 1907. He decorated his rooms in the approved style: "Curious knick-knacks, strange fruits, rare liqueurs, choice tobacco, and strange books were all around," and everything "strange and weird appealed to him."[13] He wrote home to his mother asking her to send him some pictures for the walls of his room: "a Bucklein [sic], or someone, a German artist; . . . any Burne Jones (esp. Golden Stairs) or any Leighton . . . of the Andromache of the latter I am specially fond."[14] Apart from the Classics texts he was supposed to read for Greats, he devoted most of his leisure to reading French literature, declaring a distinct preference for the Parnassian Théophile Gautier, whom he admired as much as he did the English poet Algernon Charles Swinburne.[15] In a letter to his old Uppingham friend J. T. Sedgwick, Flecker averred that Thomas Carlyle's *Sartor Resartus* was his "bible."[16]

In the spirit of bright, undergraduate facetiousness, Flecker also announced the foundation of a club called *Les Fleurs du Mal,* for which "moral turpitude [was] not necessary though desirable for membership." He declared that this organization had "a purely Praxitilian intention," was "contemplative in character, but apart from that its outlook [was] Hellenic." Early members, he declared, were "Mr. Bloom of Corpus, The Shropshire Lad and Plato."[17] Flecker's facetiousness is also apparent in a magazine which he published for Eights Week in 1906, entitled *The Best Man.* The level of its humor is strictly undergraduate; the tone of its contents is signaled by the studied brightness of the Editorial:

> Every one knows the Best Man, with his shining
> hat, his well-groomed hair, and massive
> diamond stud. For him we expunged these
> pages. We trust him not to borrow the copy
> he reads.
> Assistance has been offered to the
> editorial staff by the Suffragan Professor of
> Ontology (whose grip on reality is so tremendous),
> by a well known Peer, by a Colonial Bishop, and by
> Archibald Pottles, Esq.
> The Captain of Boats at All Souls has kindly
> revised the proofs.

The contents of *The Best Man* are an uneven mixture of undergraduate wit, lyric poetry, and serious prose, and it contains the original version of one of Flecker's more notable essays, "The Last Generation." The prevailing tone of the magazine, however, is frivolous, and among the more lighthearted contributions are several clerihews,[18] a form of verse for which Flecker had considerable talent, as these two, the most successful ones, indicate:

> I am confidential advisor
> To the Kaiser,
> Which is rather a crusher
> For the Czar of Russia

and

> When I met the Pope
> I expressed the pious hope
> That he felt quite at home
> In Rome.[19]

The Best Man was published in collaboration with Jack Beazley, with whom Flecker appears to have experienced a homosexual relationship. Beazley was Flecker's junior at Oxford by one year, coming up from Christ's Hospital in 1903, and the two men first met in February or March, 1904, at a lunch given by Frank Savery. Beazley was a handsome, literate young man with a taste for poetry and an interest in classical antiquity, which later led him to a distinguished career as an international authority on Greek vases.[20] The friendship lasted many years, and it is more than likely that Flecker's poem "The Sentimentalist," written shortly before his departure from England for the East, was addressed to his friend:

> There lies a photograph of you
> Deep in a box of broken things.
> This was a face I loved and knew
> Five years ago, when life had wings;
>
> Five years ago, when through a town
> Of bright and soft and shadowy bowers
> We walked and talked and trailed our gown
> Regardless of the cinctured hours.
>
> The precepts that we held, I kept;
> Proudly my ways with you I went:
> We lived our dreams while others slept,
> And did not shrink from sentiment.
>
> Now I go East and you stay West
> And when between us Europe lies

I shall forget what I loved best,
Away from lips and hands and eyes.

But we were Gods then: We were they
Who laughed at fools, believed in friends,
And drank to all that golden day
Before us, which this poem ends.[21]

While at Oxford Flecker also encountered the work of the more robust John Davidson. Davidson was a poor Scottish schoolmaster who, after the publication of his *Scaramouche in Naxos and Other Plays* (1889) and *In a Music Hall and Other Poems* (1891), came to London determined to make his way as a writer. At first he was moderately successful, for John Lane of the Bodley Head Press published his *Fleet Street Eclogues* (1893), *Ballads and Songs* (1894), *Fleet Street Eclogues: Second Series* (1895), and *New Ballads* (1896) in attractive, little black buckram volumes which captured the attention of readers of poetry and bibliophiles alike. By the end of the 1890s, however, Davidson's popularity had begun to decline; he found it hard to make a decent livelihood from writing; he grew embittered and paranoid. About this time, no doubt partially influenced by his waning popularity, he began to formulate a quasi-philosophical creed based on the teachings of the German philosopher Nietzsche and on the scientific writings of Charles Darwin. This creed, which glorified power and justified it in terms of the evolution of species, was expressed in a series of formless verse "testaments." These poems appealed to Flecker, as they did to many of his Oxford contemporaries, and reinforced his religious doubts, which had continued to grow since his Uppingham days.

According to Flecker's sister, James considered Davidson to be a man "in open revolt against the doctrine of the 'correct thing.' The first step to be won was freedom of self-expression," or so it seemed; "it became the one object worthy of ambition; consistency of conduct and a well-regulated life were scorned as the refuge of the unintellectual and moral coward." But, as Flecker's sister observed, "in the eagerness of his attempts, a man was apt to confuse his search for himself and his search for truth,"[22] and to some degree this is what happened to James, as his two essays on Davidson clearly show. Nevertheless, Davidson provoked the serious side of Flecker's nature, and it was not long before he declared himself to be an agnostic.

At Uppingham, he had already begun to backslide. Writing to his mother, he had announced that he was not going to attend Communion, as it seemed to him "unprofitable" to go more than once or twice a term;[23] and on October 27, 1901, he had written home at considerable length to explain in detail his disenchantment with religion as practiced at school: "Take prayer meetings first: take say the — prayer meeting. I attended it once right through a term. I now analyze my reasons for attending it. My reason was, I found, not to obtain help; nor did I go there because I enjoyed praising God. No: I went there simply because I had a vague idea I would go to heaven if I attended prayer meetings, and please you at the same time." Consequently, he wrote, he did not feel he was getting much guidance from his religious observances, especially since the people responsible for conducting these prayer meetings had little to say about the meaning of Christianity, or even about the desirability of doing good works. Instead, their idea seemed to be that one should be a very enthusiastic Christian, set a good example, and be assured of going to heaven. "Admittedly," he continued, "the continual firing of texts into my ears, which the firers did not understand any more than I did, resulted in good resolutions" which lasted for two or three days; but their "parrot-like repetition," coupled with the "silly prattle of a young curate," was hardly likely to inspire Flecker with endurable notions of the significance and worth of Christianity.[24]

Understandably, this letter caused some pain to Flecker's parents. His father was inflexible on religious belief; and more than likely Flecker's independent spirit was provoked by his father's dogmatism and by his unyielding, unquestioning faith. What is certain, however, is that Flecker's determination not to accept Christianity on trust hardened; and, as he grew to intellectual maturity, he moved increasingly nearer to the agnostic's position. By late 1903, one year after his arrival at Oxford, he was a declared agnostic; and in a letter to his father which, unfortunately, seems to have been lost, he announced his inability to accept wholeheartedly the Christian faith. His father's reply, however, has survived; and it reveals the certitude of Dr. Flecker's belief as well as his determination to prevent his son from what he regarded as an irrevocable lapse. He pointed out to his son that even men of "large intellectual power" sometimes made "astounding mistakes"; and he suggested that ordinary men, "anxious to find out the truth," have a greater chance of finding it than those whose strong intellect enslaves them. "The doctrine shall be revealed to those who are prepared to do the will," wrote Dr. Flecker, "so that if a man — if you — should take the Beatitudes as the law of life and determinedly obey them, the question of dogma might wait." Furthermore, he continued, "the trend of the best scientific thought during the last ten years has distinctly been against the attitude of 25 years ago, 'miracles are impossible'."[25]

Although, as this letter reveals, a rift now existed between Flecker and his parents, their inability to appreciate and understand his religious doubts did not preclude their capability to accept their son's comparative failure in the examinations leading to his B.A. degree. Their sympathy, no doubt comforting to Flecker, did little, however, to help him overcome his disappointment. He knew that his intellectual capabilities were above average; his friends acknowledged his superior attainments; but his poor degree placed a serious obstacle in the way of an academic career. He was forced to take stock and reconsider his future. Until now life had been pleasant and full of promise; and, though Flecker regained some of his optimism and natural ebullience, he had to realize that life, after all, was something more than a game.

III *Interval*

Flecker moved to London in the summer of 1906 to assume a teaching position at Mr. Simmons' School, Holly Hill, Hampstead. After his fiasco in the Oxford examinations, his parents had thought that the home civil service might be an appropriate career for him; but, as Jack Beazley indicated, Flecker's impetuous spirit was hardly suited to the mindless drudgery which a post in the home civil service entailed.[26] Some of his friends seemed to feel that literary journalism would be a better choice; but, rather surprisingly, he chose the teaching profession instead.

Though Flecker held rather disparaging views about schoolteachers as a class,[27] he was nonetheless interested in the theory of education, as his later treatise "The Grecians" reveals. Temperamentally, he was far from suited to the role of schoolmaster; but he appears to have been a moderate success at Mr. Simmons' school; and, according to Douglas Goldring, he "made a great and lasting impression on some of his pupils."[28] This statement, however, is probably an exaggeration since Flecker stayed with Mr. Simmons for only one term. Afterwards he taught at Mill Hill School, also in London; but, finding the heavy nonconformist atmosphere there antipathetic, he resigned to take another post at Aysgarth in the West Riding of Yorkshire, which he left in the spring of 1908, to enter the consular service.

Obviously, Flecker was not the type to be a schoolmaster. Though somewhat chastened by his indifferent success at Oxford, he was still very much the bright young man who was impetuous, frivolous, vain, impatient with routine, and eager for adventure. Goldring recalls a visit at this time to Flecker who was preparing to make a journey to France "to investigate the rising among the Vignerons of the Bordeaux district, where Catholicism was in conflict with the Republic — a romantic adventure, with revolvers in it." According to Goldring, though Flecker professed to be "packing up" and had even purchased a revolver as part of his traveling equipment, his preparations for departure were not very far advanced:

The tables and all the chairs were piled with books — beautifully bound classical texts, French and Italian novels in paper covers, copies of 'L'Assiette au Beurre," and of "Jugend," dictionaries of the poets — and, half-buried among the piles, were such things as a typewriter, a bottle of Maraschino and another of Chianti, tumblers, pictures, manuscripts. Pictures were piled up against the skirting-boards, or lay on their faces on the floor in imminent danger of being crushed under their owner's feet as he paced up and down the room.[29]

The Bordeaux adventure appears to have been postponed, for Flecker went in May, 1908, to Cambridge.[30] A few months previously, perhaps encouraged by the appearance in the fall of 1907 of *The Bridge of Fire*, his first volume of poems, he had gone to Oxford with the idea of establishing himself as a literary journalist; but, realizing at last that such a career would provide him at best with only a modest livelihood, he decided to join the consular service, hoping for a post in Greece or in what was then known as the Ottoman Empire.[31]

IV *Cambridge*

Flecker entered Caius College, Cambridge, to study Oriental languages in preparation for the student-interpretorship examination, a necessary preliminary to entering the consular service. He was certainly happy there, but he not surprisingly was unable to recapture the gaiety of his Oxford days. Dr. C. E. Raven, onetime dean of Emmanuel College, Cambridge, and also one of Flecker's old Uppingham acquaintances, presents a somewhat unflattering portrait of the poet at this time:

It was as regards affectation and self-consciousness that I noticed the greatest change in Flecker, when six years after seeing him at Uppingham he was suddenly brought into the Bachelors' Common Room at Caius, and introduced to me by the Dean. He was still brilliantly original, still arresting in his outlook: he had a very wide knowledge of things and books, especially of the obscurer sides of the classical tradition and literature; he was very greatly developed in the extent of his abilities and in power of expression; but he seemed to me to have lost the spontaneity and directness of his school-time.

He had become consciously a rebel, and consciously a genius — and the effect had been wholly bad. His criticism of men and things was no longer (I think) instinctive and true, because it was now apt to be affected. At school he never posed: at Cambridge, though he was a model of sincerity by the side of many of his contemporaries, he was no longer unconscious of the desire to produce an effect, or unwilling to give way to it.[32]

The atmosphere of Cambridge at this time was unlikely to encourage Flecker to show the better side of his personality. As Dr. Raven describes the environment, "Conventional standards in morals and religion had for the time broken down badly: the 'New Hellenism' of Lowes Dickinson and Gilbert Murray was fashionable, and with it came an outburst of abnormality and a revival of something like the aestheticism of the 'nineties."[33] A place in which posturing, affectation, and eccentricity could thrive, Flecker succumbed to its influence.

Among the poet's more colorful contemporaries was Oscar Browning, a professor of history, who displayed a crucifix on the wall to "fwighten the agnoggers," and about whom it was said that he had awakened at five one morning "and read Coventry Patmore slap through."[34] Baron Corvo (a pseudonym used by Frederick William Rolfe), a homosexual litterateur who was a rejected candidate for the priesthood, was also there; at this time he was collaborating with Father Robert Hugh Benson, himself a notable eccentric, on a book about St. Thomas of Canterbury.[35] Ronald Firbank, the frail dilettante who wrote several amusing, salacious novels in excessively mannered prose, was also there. Among such company the temptation to seek easy notoriety by way of a markedly abnormal behavior must have been strong, and it is more than likely that Flecker succumbed, hoping thereby to distinguish himself from his more conventional colleagues.

There is no evidence, however, for believing that Flecker became a self-conscious disciple of Uranian love, engaging in homoerotic relationships similar to that which he enjoyed at Oxford with Jack Beazley. Indeed, there is some doubt whether his relationship with Beazley could be clinically defined as homosexual. There are, after all, an infinite number of gradations between the Platonic affection of Alfred Lord Tennyson for Arthur Hallam, recorded in "In Memoriam," and Oscar Wilde's passion for stable boys and news vendors, which found expression in the stained bed sheets of the Cadogan Hotel. Where a close friendship between men passes from the nobly Platonic to the socially unacceptable is hard to define. And in Flecker's time it was not unusual for young men at the universities to enjoy intense, self-involving affairs with members of their own sex. There is no doubt, however, that Flecker was sexually abnormal, and later, when he married, whipping became an essential ingredient of sexual relations with his wife.[36]

Possibly it was this side of Flecker's nature which brought him a measure of notoriety. Equally probable, however, it was Flecker's talent for obscenity which brought him into disrepute with the more conservative elements at Cambridge. Goldring maintains that Flecker's obscenity amounted to a gift, and many of his famous witticisms and jeux d'esprit (written down and illustrated in a MS volume, bound in "art linen," called the "Yellow Book of Japes," the joint production of Flecker and his greatest Oxford friend) are scarcely likely to find their way into print.[37] Another of his friends recalls that his most vivid recollections of Flecker were his "jokes, limericks, rhymes, and fantastic social schemes which were never meant to pass beyond word of mouth," one of the more repeatable being a campaign for the compulsory deflowering of Cambridge women students by a strictly professional staff kept for this purpose.[38] What seems most likely, therefore, is that Flecker at Cambridge, as at Oxford, aspired with a greater degree of self-consciousness to the role of enfant terrible. At Oxford, he was able to maintain the pose with high-spirited vigor; at Cambridge, having lost the prerogative of youth, his behavior was barely tolerable.

Most acquaintances seemed to feel that Flecker was out of place at Cambridge; he remained "typically Oxonian to the end."[39] Writing home to his mother, he remarked that, "under the heading 'Derelict,' the editor of *The Granta* (whom I met at dinner the other night) is publishing an editorial on me (quite absurd) as the typical Oxford man!!!" The editorial appeared in the May 30, 1908, issue. Not an especially incisive portrait of Flecker, it is interesting in so far as it draws attention to the degree to which he eventually stood out against his surroundings, and as it indicates the impact he made on other people. To the editor of *The Granta*, Flecker was a shallow, somewhat pompous poseur who was destined "to drink port and propound brilliantly superficial epigrams for all eternity."[40]

The atmosphere at Cambridge during Flecker's time has been realistically portrayed by Shane Leslie in his novel *The Cantab* in which he emphasizes the prevailing tendency toward Estheticism, but at the same time draws attention to a growing awareness of social responsibility.[41] Flecker, though he struck most people as being no more than an Esthete, was also a Fabian, a member of that political group which sought social equality by way of quietly persuasive argument rather than by a revolt of the masses. The Cambridge University Fabian Society had been founded in 1907 with V. H. Mottram as president and with J. C. Squire, poet and editorial successor to Edward Marsh of the Georgian poetry anthologies, as secretary. The majority of the members were earnest and dedicated — Hugh Dalton, later chancellor of the exchequer in the post-World War II Labour cabinet, was one of the earliest to join. Much high-spirited ragging occurred; and, in their insistence on wearing working-class cloth caps and studiously casual attire, they were almost as guilty of affectation as the Esthetes.[42] Therefore, though Flecker seems to have been moderately sympathetic to the cause of social equality, one should not place too much emphasis on his association with the Fabians: to be a socialist was original, and also a lark.

Flecker was certainly a less sincere Fabian than Rupert Brooke, the young Georgian poet who died of septicaemia shortly after Flecker himself and with whom he became acquainted early in 1908. Both were members of the Fabian Society; and, though they both attended Sidney and Beatrice Webb's Fabian Society summer school at Llanbedr, Wales, their relationship was far from cordial.[43] At this particular school the theme for discussion was the idea that "the Universal maintenance of a definite minimum of civilised life becomes the joint responsibility of an indissoluble partnership in which the individual and the community have reciprocal duties."[44] It is unlikely, however, that Flecker took an interested part in the discussion; his attention seems to have been directed more towards a slim, Burne-Jones type of girl, Eleanor Finlayson, with whom he was soon contemplating an "indissoluble union" other than that which the Webbs had in mind.[45] With characteristic impulsiveness, Flecker proposed to her; she accepted; but the engagement was later broken. Their temperaments were too divergent to hold much promise of a lasting relationship.[46]

As at Oxford, Flecker participated in numerous extracurricular activities; he also had a fairly intense social life. He spoke at several university debates and spent endless hours punting on the River Cam. He wrote poetry and some prose — though rather less than he had at Oxford[47] — and he studied Turkish, Persian, and Arabic in preparation for his student-interpreter's examination. At last, he was able to write home that examinations were over: "Feel very blissful — exam. all over: did fairly well considering my small knowledge: afraid the vivas did not go off very well. Worked twelve hours a day during exam: six hours exam, six hours work."[48] He soon left Cambridge, a place he had never really cared for;[49] and he embarked in June, 1910, for Constantinople where he had been appointed vice consul.

CHAPTER 2

Flecker Abroad

I Constantinople

WHEN Flecker arrived in Constantinople toward the end of
June or early July, 1910, he was eager to assume his duties as
a vice consul. Although he was forced in a sense to join the foreign
service, having recognized that he was ill-suited to become a
schoolmaster and that the chances of his success as a literary journalist were slim, Flecker's decision to make a career in the Middle
East as one of His Majesty's consuls was not especially surprising.
The British have long been fascinated by the Eastern Mediterranean
area and by the Arabian peninsula, as numerous travel narratives
from the Medieval Sir John Mandeville to the contemporary
Lawrence Durrell testify. It is true that Sir Richard Burton complained of the lack of respect accorded to Orientalists by his fellow
Victorians,[1] and even in Flecker's day Frank Harris felt justified in
complaining that "the crass ignorance [of England] concerning the
Oriental peoples which should most interest her, exposes her to the
contempt of Europe as well as of the Eastern World."[2] One should
not forget, however, that in Victorian England *The Arabian Nights*
was second in popularity only to the Bible;[3] and, as far as the British
government was concerned, the Middle East was an important area
of its foreign policy, a vital link in the route to India, a country
described in the report that inaugurated the Committee of Imperial
Defence in 1904 as ranking next after the British Navy as a compo-
nent of British strength.[4]

Therefore, when Flecker went to Constantinople, diplomatic
attention was focused on the Middle East; but comparatively few
people seemed to have known much about it — and what little they
did know was derived from *The Arabian Nights* rather than from
eyewitness accounts or from firsthand knowledge. To most people, it

35

was an exotic fairyland which promised endless thrills, glamor, and high adventure. It is not surprising, then, that Flecker's romantic spirit should have responded to the East, prompting him to make a career there. He had long been fascinated by this part of the world, and his literary tastes tended toward the exotic — he much preferred Tennyson's "The Lotus Eaters" to his "In Memoriam"[5] — and in his youth George Borrow, author of *Lavengro* and *The Bible in Spain*, strongly appealed to him.[6] While at school, Flecker even went to the trouble of copying out Sir Richard Burton's oriental poem *Kasidah* since it was difficult to obtain at the time.[7] Furthermore, his hair and complexion were dark — there was a Jewish heritage from his father's side — and he wrote in 1905 to his mother from Oxford with evident relish: "Somebody, I don't know who, wanted to know who that 'Saturnine Oriental' was the other day."[8] There is little doubt, therefore, that Flecker was strongly predisposed to enjoy working in the Middle East; and, when he went ashore at Constantinople, his spirits were high.

Flecker's vice-consular tasks at Constantinople seem to have been light. Although Britain's presence in the Ottoman Empire was regarded as crucial — "Turkey is as good a guardian of the route to India as any Arab would be," Lord Palmerston had said [9] — this significance seems to have had little effect on the work Flecker was called upon to do. He took rooms at Candilli, where he could look across the Bosphorus to Roumali Hissar and indulge his romantic tendencies "till the brown Castle walls turned gold, and the blue sea white and wet, till the sun went down not amid the patches and pageantry of our Northern settings, but gently leaving a sky as softly coloured as the petal of a rose."[10] Even after a few months, however, he was beginning to find the place oppressive; and, though he was able to admire the beauty of his exotic surroundings, he longed to see a "slag-heap or a gaswork, or any strong, bold, ugly thing to break the spell of this terrible and malignant beauty that saps body and soul."[11] Already his dream was turning sour.

Flecker's restless northern spirit was unable to come to terms with the static richness of his surroundings; and once, when riding in a Constantinople bus (lately the property of London Transport), he thrilled at the sight of "golden words" behind the driver's seat: "names of places half-forgotten and long desired, Oxford Circus, Marble Arch, Edgware Road and Cricklewood." Then, "like a chime of silver, distant bells, or some sweet poem of a fickle lover who has strung together the names of his mistresses and loves, whispers in

[his] ear this table of fares in the old Vanguard motor-bus, till [he] could weep for the bitterness of [his] exile and [his] great desire for London Town and English faces; for the thunder of Charing Cross and the cries of Oxford Circus, for the sweep of Regent Street, for the glory of a great Empire and the fellowship of men."[12]

Flecker's love for the East was little more than a romantic infatuation, neither profound nor long lasting. It was one thing to dream of sandal-footed maids in flowing, gauze draperies, of delicate-featured young men, and of the opulent ceremony of *The Arabian Nights;* it was something else to confront Eastern reality. Though Flecker continued to be fascinated by his exotic environment, he also began to detest it; and, as time passed, his nostalgia for home increased.

He had, of course, compensations. His colleagues were congenial; and Sir Reader Bullard, his immediate superior, was an agreeable, literate man with whom Flecker got on tolerably well.[13] He went swimming, riding, picnicking; he played tennis; he read books that had long remained on his shelves unopened; and he did some writing, his most notable achievement of this time being his *The Scholars' Italian Book* (1911). Then, in September, after swimming in the Black Sea, he caught a chill which developed into a fever. When a doctor was called in, Flecker was informed after a careful medical examination that he had tuberculosis. He was granted sick leave almost immediately, and he was in England once more at the end of the month; there he consulted a specialist who advised a three-month period in a sanitarium, followed by six months' rest.

Flecker was hospitalized at Cranham in the Cotswolds, not far from Cheltenham; and, making good use of his enforced leisure, he wrote the first draft of one of his best poems, "Oak and Olive." Flecker soon persuaded both himself and his doctors that he was completely cured; and, believing that the prescribed six months of rest was unnecessary, he went off to Paris where he awaited news of an expected appointment at Smyrna (modern Izmir). In Paris, he finished his play *Don Juan,* begun at Cranham, and sent it to George Bernard Shaw for an opinion as to its merit. Shaw was moderately impressed, and Flecker returned to London and tried, unsuccessfully, to have it staged.[14] Meanwhile, he continued to write poetry, added six pieces to the previously published *Thirty-Six Poems,* and re-issued the volume with revisions in 1911 under the title *Forty-Two Poems.*

By March 31, 1911, Flecker, back in Constantinople, heard definitely that he would be transferred to Smyrna. The following

month he announced his forthcoming marriage to Hellé Skiardaressi, a Greek lady whom he had met on board the ship that had
first taken him to Constantinople, and with whose family he had
stayed in Paris after leaving Cranham; but his engagement came to
most people as a surprise. Not only had his engagement to Eleanor
Finlayson just been broken off, he had also become involved with a
"fluffy" little English girl called Leila Berkeley, whom he had met
while convalescing in England.[15] The prospect of Flecker's marrying
Hellé, therefore, seemed most unlikely, especially as he suffered a
relapse shortly after his arrival at Smyrna. Once again he went on
sick leave, this time to Athens. On May 25, 1911, however, the couple were wed, Flecker's health having momentarily taken a turn for
the better. They went off to Corfu for their honeymoon, during
which time he wrote several poems, most notably "A Ship, an Isle, a
Sickle Moon," and began what was to become his best-known, most
successful work, *Hassan*. Instead of returning to Smyrna, however,
he was posted to Beirut where he arrived in September to assume his
duties as vice consul.

II *Beirut*

Although Geraldine Hodgson claims that Flecker did some
"useful and excellent work" as vice consul in Beirut,[16] even the
usually circumspect *Dictionary of National Biography* admits that
Flecker was "not very efficient."[17] Irritable by nature, his dislike of
the East increasing, and now disenchanted with his consular career,
Flecker was hardly a suitable person to represent the British abroad.
A few hours after his arrival, having decided to move to Aley in the
mountains to escape the oppressive heat of coastal lowlands, he
became involved in a public argument with "a man in a fez" who
refused to add an extra first-class carriage to the train which was to
take them to their destination. After Flecker had called the man "a
dirty Turk who wanted bakshish," he discovered that he was the station master and, as he put it, "a better Christian than *vous mon-
sieur*." The quarrel was patched up, however, and Flecker obtained
his first-class carriage to Aley.[18] Not long afterwards, he was again
the center of a violent scene while staying with his wife at what used
to be The German Hotel, now long since disappeared, where he
engaged in a bout of fisticuffs with a Russian diplomat over the use
of a common hall that separated their apartments, an incident which
almost became a scandal.[19]

To Flecker, Beirut was a "hole"; and the "respectable people" at

the consulate were tiresome and unpleasant.[20] Writing to John
Mavrogordato, previously a reader for the publishing house of J. M.
Dent, and at this time subeditor of the *English Review*, Flecker announced: "I live here in clear sunshine among damned fools. Both of
us are a bit sick of Beirut."[21] When he was not openly hostile to the
people surrounding him, he seems to have masked his feelings with
irony, as his account of an affray provoked by the Druses of Sharoun
and another of the Italian bombardment reveal. Describing the
Druse affair, Flecker writes:

A much respected old gentleman of the tribe had been grievously wounded
by a hand unknown on his way from Brumana; hence the Druses were
assembling in their secret places crying for Christian blood; and hence the
Christians of the valley, led by some brawny returned emigrants from
America, had had all the church bells rung as a summons to all Christians to
gather in force. A good scrap is still considered to be better than litigation in
Lebanon — and, after all, what is Lebanese Justice unless you've got a consul to doctor your case? A woman accused of stealing a hen will fly to Russia
or France for protection. A Druse appeals to England, who once preserved
them from a richly merited punishment at the hands of the French for their
massacring ways. The English public was persuaded by a venal press that a
Druse was a kind of Protestant suffering martyrdom at the hands of
papistical Maronites.

The affair was finally resolved by the intervention of the British consul general, "who accomplished it with all the skill of one ac-
customed to Oriental incidents," calmed the "wildest spirits," and
settled the whole business shortly before midnight.[22]
    In describing the Italian bombardment of Beirut, which took
place in February, 1912, Flecker also resorts to irony, making the incident appear like a scene from a comic opera, though in reality it
was serious enough as accounts by other eye witnesses make clear.[23]
He describes how "one spring morning" he was wakened by the
report of a cannon from two Italian cruisers which were endeavoring
to sink a Turkish gunboat and how the Italians by mistake sent five
shells into the town, hitting two banks. He continues:

About a hundred interested spectators on the quay, struck by the bursting
shells, paid the penalty of their rashness. As for the Turks, no watch had
been kept on the boat; the officers all slept onshore and only a few reached
the ship in time. But they refused to surrender and pluckily mis-directed
several shells all round the harbour, till their little biscuit-tin was sunk up to

its funnels. The attempt made by some gallant Arab boatmen to sink the cruisers by rifle fire failed completely. They had been persuaded, ever since the day of the Camperdown disaster off Tripoli in Syria, that you had only to puncture an ironclad and it would disappear.

Meanwhile, wrote Flecker, there was considerable excitement in the town. "At the first shots, the howling Arabs fled indoors in senseless panic"; but they quickly recovered, "looted the barracks and attempted to murder all Christians." The crowd became increasingly belligerent, and Flecker was soon surrounded; but he was rescued at last by a Turkish soldier who escorted him back to his hotel.[24]

The Druse affray and the Italian bombardment were the two most notable incidents during Flecker's stay in Beirut, both of which he was able to view with the detached irony of one whom T. E. Lawrence described as being a "furiously British, patriotic, God save the King exile."[25] The truth is that — in spite of his much vaunted understanding of the East[26] and his familiarity with some of its languages — Flecker had little or no sympathy for the Arabs or for the country in which he was living. He enjoyed the scenery around Beirut; he wrote appreciatively of some of the local beauty spots — the Dog River, the Beirut River valley, Byblos — describing them in picturesque terms in letters home to his parents;[27] but his friends tended to be drawn from the British or from the sizeable American colony. No record exists of his having been on even moderately intimate terms with anyone who came from the eastern part of the Mediterranean, even though his wife was Greek. He carried out his duties with little competence and with no real enthusiasm; his main concerns were literary.

By reading and writing, Flecker could keep his environment at a safe distance; and, though his official duties necessitated his involvement in Lebanese affairs, there was always the possibility of escape into literature. It was not that Flecker's artistic temperament was unable to accommodate itself to governmental responsibility — as, for example, seems to have been the situation with Lawrence Durrell in Cairo and in Alexandria.[28] Rather, Flecker's essential Englishness made him feel alienated from his surroundings; he was much less of an exotic than he thought. Through literature, however, he could keep in touch with the cultivated world of Oxbridge and literary London — maintain contact with a way of life that meant more to him than anything else in the world, more, it seems, than even his marriage.

In 1912, the Fleckers moved into a picturesque, red-roofed house in the village of Areiya, not far from Aley and some distance above sea level; and this house, incidentally, still stands, situated near a Druse tomb which, according to local legend, Flecker frequently visited.[29] There they were visited by T. E. Lawrence, whom Flecker described in a letter to Frank Savery of January 10, 1912, as "a strange boy who tramps Syria on foot and digs Hittites for Hogarth" — a reference to Lawrence's involvement in the Karkamesh archaeological dig in Syria, which preceded his better known role as one of the prime movers of the Arab revolt.[30] Lawrence did not stay with the Fleckers very long — probably for no more than two or three days — but it was long enough for him to form a shrewd judgment of the poet, which he expressed in a brief though perceptive essay published many years later.

Lawrence gloried in his facility to forget his Englishness and to adapt himself to Arab civilization, the more primitive the better;[31] therefore, he was somewhat contemptuous of Flecker's inability to do the same. In some ways, however, the two men were similar: both held romantic notions about the mysterious East; both were sensitive men of action with literary aspirations. They differed, however, in that Lawrence, a visionary megalomaniac, had the will to force his dream to become reality; Flecker, less intense and uncommitted to any specific program or ideology, found that his dream was better left as a dream since he could not cope with reality. As Lawrence wrote, "By instinct, by taste, by upbringing, by inheritance, [Flecker's] was the town-life of rich Syria, the satins and silks, perfumes, sweet-meats, grocers and Syrian boys. Dim-skinned, dark-haired musicians. Ah, if he could have thought of these in the next street but one. In the next street he grew sated with the nearness of them. In his street — he longed for Marlborough Downs."[32]

The consular service is not the place for dreamers, particularly those who dream continually of home; and, not surprisingly, Flecker's relationship with his superiors at the consulate in Beirut became increasingly strained. To some degree, this was not his fault because his health began to deteriorate rapidly, disabling him from carrying out his official duties as well as he might. He also failed a required examination in Turkish. Much to the annoyance of Consul General Cumberbatch, Flecker requested and obtained leave from Beirut on the grounds of ill health.

He returned to England, and he appeared on November 29 at the Admiralty office where he hoped to enlist Edward Marsh's support in an attempt to find other employment than in the consular service.[33] Marsh, describing the event in a letter to Rupert Brooke, revealed that he was not especially inclined toward Flecker; and he gave no indication that he would be involved in a few months' time in one of the most time-consuming and difficult editorial projects he was ever to undertake, advising Flecker on the revision of *Hassan*. "Flecker turned up at the Admiralty for a short time this morning," wrote Marsh. "He has just arrived from Syria which bores him stiff, and he was off to see [Sir Walter] Raleigh and try to get a professorship of Literature out of him. There is much to be said against his exterior, but I hope to see him more at length when he comes back, and to get over it."[34] Flecker soon returned, bringing a copy of *Hassan* with him, which he showed to Marsh, who offered to take it along to Harley Granville-Barker, the dramatist and actor-manager, in the hope of getting it staged.[35] At the same time, Flecker pressed Marsh to use his influence with A. C. Benson and the Cambridge Appointments Board to try to find him suitable employment which would enable him to leave the consular service. Marsh complied, but the response from Benson was not very encouraging. He admitted that he found Flecker "an interesting creature, with a sort of curious and rather attractive wildness about him"; but he added: "To speak plainly, a man who writes fine poetry, has married a Greek wife, and wants to throw up a consular post, is difficult to place . . . the same sort [of difficulty] as there would have been in placing Shelley."[36]

Meanwhile, Flecker had decided to file an application for a transfer to the general consular service, which would have meant his removal from Beirut. His request, dated December 10, 1912, and written from his father's home at Dean Close, Cheltenham, summarizes his reasons for requesting the transfer. He claimed that "circumstances over which [he] had no control" militated against his passing his examination in Turkish, and he felt that he was unlikely to pass it at the next sitting. He also pointed out that his health, "permanently enfeebled at Constantinople," made it impossible for him to accept a post in the Levant service; and, since the capture of Tripoli and the possible partition of Macedonia, it was probable that fewer consuls with a knowledge of Turkish would be required. Furthermore, his illness had imposed a severe strain on his financial resources; as a result, he would not be able to return to Beirut without an outfit allowance and traveling expenses. Finally, and most significantly, he asserted that "I feel myself seriously unfitted by temperament for life in the East."[37]

Flecker's request was forwarded to the Foreign Office together with a confidential report from the private secretary. The report is interesting reading, as it is clear that by this time everyone was convinced that the sooner Flecker left the consular service the better it would be for all concerned. The substance of this report is as follows:

At the end of Mr. Flecker's first year at Cambridge we received adverse reports as to his attendance at lectures and his progress. He was informed that unless some improvement was shown, the question of whether it would be possible to retain his services would have to be considered.

Subsequently he improved greatly and passed first at his final exam. Professor Browne stated that he had made extraordinary progress, that he was undoubtedly very clever, and that he had really exerted himself.

Mr. Flecker's Intermediate examn. as an Assistant was postponed owing to his ill-health, and when it took place the result was unsatisfactory, although allowance had to be made for ill health. Mr. Flecker's Turkish was bad, and his papers in Ottoman law revealed a very insufficient study of that subject, which he was required to take again at his final examination.

Mr. Flecker's final examn. was unsatisfactory, and even allowing for ill-health the examiner could not recommend that he should be adjudged to have passed. It was recognized that he had not good facilities for acquiring Turkish at Beirut. He again did badly in Ottoman law.

I do not think Mr. Flecker will ever make a satisfactory officer, and in any case his request for a transfer to the General Service should not be entertained.

I suggest that we should inform him our warning was only addressed to him after a full consideration of the extenuating circumstances in his case. We might also point out that his work in Ottoman law as well as in the Turkish language was unsatisfactory. Say that his request for a transfer to the General Service cannot be entertained. Grant extension of leave.

Appended to the private secretary's report is an even more negative, typewritten note, presumably by someone at the Foreign Office: "Mr. Flecker says he cannot accept any of the unhealthy posts in the Levant and therefore, presumably, he will also be unable to accept posts of the like nature in the General Consular Service. These 'invalid' Vice-Consuls are a great nuisance to us and I would not like to see another added to our list. Mr. Marling in a private letter has spoken of Mr. Flecker as being physically a wretched 'crock.' He had much better resign." This note is followed by two terse statements: "I quite agree," in one hand, and "I agree too," in another.[38]

For the time being, however, Flecker remained in the service of the Crown. He had not the slightest inclination to return to Beirut, and the consular service was not eager to have him either. In the closing days of 1912, · Flecker wrote to his father: "I am so disheartened. It is my tragedy. I have got to go back to Beirut alone, possibly to die. No one will do anything for me. . . . If you had the slightest idea of the difficulties of living in the East as we have tried, with no fixed home, and with a most serious illness! Till I have a good situation in England I cannot do well financially, and shall never have a moment's happiness or peace of mind."[39]

Nevertheless, he returned to Beirut, but his health was deteriorating rapidly, and he seemed on the verge of a nervous breakdown. As he wrote home toward the end of February, 1913, "Under no condition whatever, for no consideration on earth, will I remain in this Service for another year. The place drives me mad."[40] A month later, his health broke down once more; and this time there was serious cause for alarm. On March 14, 1913, he wrote home to his mother: "All hope of anything, of seeing England again, ever having a home or a happy day again, I have utterly abandoned."[41]

Meanwhile, Flecker was still writing poetry; and many pieces he produced during his short stay in Beirut are among the best he ever composed. "Areiya," for example, is a delicate touching lyric inspired by the house the Fleckers rented in the mountains, one of his few seemingly genuine love poems.[42] The tone of this piece is tranquil and contented, but he gives expression more frequently in other poems to his unhappiness and nostalgia for home. "In Hospital," for example, written a month or so before Flecker left Beirut, is full of weariness and despair:

> Would I might lie like this, without the pain,
> For seven years — as one with snowy hair,
> Who in the high tower dreams his dying reign —
>
> Lie here and watch the walls — how grey and bare,
> The metal bed-post, the uncoloured screen,
> The mat, the jug, the cupboard, and the chair;
>
> And served by an old woman, calm and clean,
> Her misted face familiar, yet unknown,
> Who comes in silence, and departs unseen,
>
> And with no other visit, lie alone,
> Nor stir, except I had my food to find
> In that dull bowl Diogenes might own.

And down my window I would draw the blind,
And never look without, but, waiting, hear
A noise of rain, a whistling of the wind,

And only know that flame-foot Spring is near
By trilling birds, or by the patch of sun
Crouching behind my curtain. So, in fear,

Noon dreams should enter, softly, one by one,
And throng about the floor, and float and play
And flicker on the screen, while minutes run —

The last majestic minutes of the day —
And with the mystic shadows, shadow grow.
Then the grey square of wall should fade away,

And glow again, and open, and disclose
The shimmering lake in which the planets swim,
And all that lake a dewdrop on a rose.[43]

After Flecker's release from the hospital where this poem was written, he moved into a small, furnished house rented to them by a professor of what used to be the Syrian Protestant College but after 1920 became the American University of Beirut. Toward the end of April, however, he was ordered by his doctor to go to the mountains where, accompanied by his wife, he moved into a hotel in Brumana where he stayed until the latter part of May. During this time, he wrote "Brumana," a desperately nostalgic piece which aptly summarizes the poet's onetime romantic longing for exotic climes and his subsequent disillusionment. The poem begins with a typically Georgian evocation of the English countryside, somewhat reminiscent of Rupert Brooke's "The Old Vicarage: Grantchester," a poem which similarly contrasts the tranquil charm of English rural life with an alien environment.[44] Flecker writes:

O shall I never be home again?
Meadows of England shining in the rain
Spread wide your daisied lawns: your ramparts green
With briar fortify, with blossom screen
Till my far morning — and O streams that slow
And pure and deep through plains and playlands go,
For me all your love and all your kingcups store,
And — dark militia of the southern shore,
Old Fragrant friends — preserve me the last lines

> Of that long saga which you sung me, pines,
> When, lonely boy, beneath the chosen tree
> I listened, with my eyes upon the sea.

But, says Flecker, those "traitor pines" sang what life has found "the falsest of fair tales." He dreamed of "lands where blaze the unimaginable flowers"; but, when he actually was among them, the dream was more appealing than the reality. The "gossip pines" of the hills around Brumana still have the power to speak to him, but they now whisper thoughts of home that fill him with memories of the countryside around Bournemouth:

> Tis ever sweet to lie
> On the dry carpet of the needles brown,
> And though the fanciful green lizard stir
> And windy odours light as thistledown
> Breathe from the lavdanon and lavender,
> Half to forget the wandering and pain,
> Half to remember days that have gone by,
> And dream and dream that I am home again.[45]

Poor Flecker was never to return home again. Instead, he was advised to enter a sanitarium; he left Beirut; and in June, 1913, he was admitted to the Leysin sanitarium in Switzerland.

III   *Switzerland*

Almost immediately after being admitted at Leysin, Flecker's health began to improve; and, with that unfounded optimism which was characteristic of him throughout his life, he began to plan the future. He took a keen interest in the controversy surrounding the appointment of the new poet laureate; and, when he wrote to *The Daily Chronicle* recommending Rudyard Kipling, the newspaper published his letter on June 11, 1913.[46] He worked at *Hassan,* and his letters at this time are full of references to his literary ambitions and of wry comments on the unprofitability of literary production. Although still employed by the consular service — it had, in fact, allowed him an extension of sick leave — Flecker knew he would never serve as an officer again; he had also vowed never again to be a schoolmaster, even if his health proved equal to such employment.[47] The only other possible alternative was writing, and to it he directed all his efforts. He requested books from home and a puppet theater to help him in revising *Hassan,* which he slowly molded into its final form. In July, 1913, he published his volume of poems *The Golden Journey to Samarkand;* he sent home for the manuscript of his play *Don Juan,* with the intention of reworking it; and, by the end of the year, he had read proofs of his novel *The King of Alsander,* which was published in March, 1914.

The improvement in Flecker's health was short-lived; he suffered a relapse which forced him to realize that chances of recovery were remote. The foreign service, however, kept him on at half salary, which relieved him of considerable financial strain; and, still anxious to leave his mark as a writer, he began, at the suggestion of Douglas Goldring, an English translation of Virgil's *Aeneid.*[48] By this time, he had been moved to another sanitarium at Davos, also in Switzerland; and his letters to his family and friends became increasingly punctuated with expressions of exasperation and misery as the pain and discomfort of his illness intensified.

In August, 1914, war was declared; and, though Flecker's condition was such that he now found great difficulty in even writing, he took an active interest in the early stages of the war, especially in the moral issues which the war brought into focus. Writing to his mother in September, for example, he said:

You know I love and venerate France. Why do you therefore write irritating disparagements of the French generals who have done so magnificently? No nation but the French (I admit we have given splendid help) could ever have stood up to the Germans like that — and the French, about whom I know a vast amount, have achieved this result through the great writers who have been preaching unanimity, Christianity, and discipline in France for the last ten years. I have never heard anyone accuse the generals of mistakes. The Italian military experts consider the retreat on Paris as a marvellous feat.

Again, you must remember that men like Bernard Shaw and myself (I have not the Xtian virtue of intellectual modesty, I admit) are more likely to be right than Roseberry. Of course, it is very easy to agree with Roseberry, who very ably and sweetly says nothing whatever in several columns. But do you *know* anything about this Belgian business (eg. the date of the treaty and who signed it). We have torn up bits of paper enough ourselves — Heaven knows — we let Austria enslave Bosnia, which we had guaranteed many years later than Belgium, without a word. Vile hypocrisy. We went to war because we had a moral obligation to France.

The Belgian business served as a useful ultimatum to Germany, who we knew twenty years ago had decided on that route — and a sop to a populace wanting something to drivel about.

Then Neitzsche. I am and always have been most anti-Nietzschen. About Christianity, do read a little Chesterton (*Orthodoxy* for instance) and the life of S. Francis or something — to see what it can mean to other people — and to me. For me that's what it means. Really there are higher forms of it than your Welsh revivalist. I am not a good Christian, and hours of bed make me impatient.[49]

This extract is worth quoting in full for several reasons. Despite his rapidly failing health — Flecker was only three months away from death — the letter indicates that he could still take an active interest in current affairs. It is also interesting for the light it throws on Flecker's interest in moral and spiritual values. To maintain that he had always been "anti-Nietzschen" is not strictly true — as an earlier disciple of John Davidson, he could hardly have failed to have accepted some of the German philosopher's views — but what is clear is that his youthful assertion of agnosticism was little more than an undergraduate gesture of bravado. True, he did not subscribe to the narrow, simplistic faith of his parents after he went to Uppingham; but he seems to the end to have remained, at least nominally, a Christian, attaching himself latterly to the "muscular Christianity" of G. K. Chesterton, which glorified social work no less than faith and ritual, and reaffirmed the heritage of rural England. Later, however, Flecker wrote somewhat unconvincingly to his mother that, though he intended to take Communion at Christmas, he "had not been suddenly converted or anything like that." He "felt the attraction of the English Church Service and Bible, and the Englishness of it all too keenly to turn to foreign creeds however much attractive."[50]

On one level, of course, Flecker's revival of faith was a nostalgic yearning for the days of his childhood, a return to the womb of sunny, well-ordered days; Sunday chapel; and the rose garden at Dean Close. Moreover, his letters home at this time are full of requests for his "loved books," those which had pleasant emotional associations for him and recalled happier times. He also wrote home for "really good cards of the Cotswolds, Gloucester Cathedral and even the horrid old town itself," adding: "You don't know how jolly I have got my bedroom — like the nursery used to be got up — with pictures without frames, beautiful 1720 maps (I had picked up in Paris for a penny years ago), photos, pictures out of the old *Studio* etc."[51]

Flecker's homesickness was intensified by the absence of friends. Before the outbreak of the war, Frank Savery, who was posted at the legation at Berne, had made frequent visits; but these were now interrupted. Though Flecker's wife was with him, he appeared to set greater store on those friendships which recalled his home in England. He kept his interest in the contemporary literary scene, and he continued to write; and a collection of the poems he wrote immediately before and at this time, *The Old Ships*, appeared posthumously in 1915. Considering Flecker's physical state, the quality of the work in this collection is remarkably good; only the content, not the technique, suggests that he was a dying man. It is interesting to note, however, that a long poem called "The Burial in England," which could so easily have been a self-pitying lament, is in fact a stirring, if somewhat sentimental, exercise in patriotism; its tone and subject matter recall a more famous poem on the same theme by Rupert Brooke, "The Soldier."[52]

Around Christmas, 1914, Flecker's health improved slightly; but the improvement was only a brief prelude before his death. On New Year's Day, he had a relapse; and on January 3, 1915, he died. He was buried in the crypt of the Anglican church at Davos; but his wife, realizing that a final resting place away from his beloved England was an inappropriate end for him, made arrangements for his body to be taken to England in a British destroyer. Conveyed to Cheltenham, it was reinterred in the cemetery on the outskirts of the town. A grey, granite cross was placed on his grave; and his wife chose a singularly apt quotation from his works as an epitaph, which is as much a testimony to her understanding of her husband's character and personality as it is to the poet himself. Taken from the last line of his poem "Hexameters," it reads quite simply: "O Lord, restore his realm to the dreamer."[53]

CHAPTER 3

The Poetry

I *Georgian or Parnassian*

B Y including several poems by Flecker in his recent anthology of Georgian poetry, James Reeves reflects the customary view of Flecker as a Georgian.[1] One can see why he should be considered a member of this group since, like many other poets of his generation, he looked instinctively to the editor of the *Georgian Poetry* anthologies, Edward Marsh, for guidance; his poetry was included in the first two of these collections, giving them, as Robert Ross has observed, added "strength and sinew";[2] and the second volume was dedicated to Flecker and Rupert Brooke. Therefore, there is nothing wrong in seeing Flecker as a Georgian who is mentioned with Walter de la Mare, Edward Thomas, J. C. Squire, John Drinkwater, and W. H. Davies, all members of the group.

Actually, the term "Georgian" is sufficiently vague to characterize almost any poet writing during the period from 1910 to 1925. The term was first used by Edward Marsh in 1912, the year of King George V's coronation when, in an introduction to an anthology of contemporary verse, he maintained that "English poetry was now once again putting on a new strength and beauty" and was about to enter "a new Georgian period which might take rank in due time with the several great poetic ages of the past." Calling his collection simply *Georgian Poetry*, Marsh also maintained that his selection had been made with "no definite aim" in mind; it was merely a representative selection of the best work available at the time.

Despite Marsh's declared avoidance of "definite aim," it was inevitable that his collection and the later ones he edited, as well as those for which J. C. Squire was responsible, should have had a distinctive character. Therefore, though, strictly speaking, there is no such thing as a "Georgian movement," the word "Georgian" does suggest a particular kind of poetry distinguishable from other poetry written at the time. Unlike the verse of the Decadent poets of the 1890s — that written by Oscar Wilde, Arthur Symons, and Ernest Dowson, for example — Georgian poetry has little nostalgia and still less wild yearning and preoccupation with sex. Unlike the verse of the so-called Counter-Decadents — Rudyard Kipling, W. E. Henley, and Sir Henry Newbolt, for example — it avoids national and patriotic themes; and little poetry in the Georgian anthologies is concerned with religion. Stylistically, most of the Georgian poets seem to have avoided self-conscious symbolism, sonorous Victorian rhythms, obscure and bizarre images and phraseology. Above all, the Georgians, harking back to the Wordsworthian tradition, seem to have been concerned with nature and with rural life.

Some of Flecker's poetry approximates this description — poems such as "Oxford Canal" and "Brumana," for example; on the other hand, most of Flecker's poetry does not.[3] The exotic setting of many of his poems; the fact that many of them are translations; the impression Flecker gives of caring more *how* he says something than *what* he says; the fact that the most clearly traceable influence on his verse is the literature of late nineteenth-century France — all these factors tend to make Flecker's poetry less characteristic of the Georgians than of the "art-for-art's-sake" school of two decades earlier, most notably those who subscribed to the Esthetic philosophy of the French Parnassians.

The doctrine of "art for art's sake" goes back at least as far as Immanuel Kant, the German philosopher, whose notion of "purposiveness without purpose" is generally held to be the germ of the idea;[4] but it first received emphatic expression in France in the writings of Théophile Gautier who, tired of the vapid platitudes of French Romanticism, declared that art was above political and social considerations; and he proceeded to demonstrate this dictum by writing poetry and novels which had little relationship with either. The Victorian critic and esthetician Walter Pater was mainly responsible for popularizing the "art-for-art's-sake" cult in England; and, though his disciples seem not always to have understood him properly, his name was frequently invoked by those who professed to believe that a work of art should be judged solely in esthetic terms. Believing that art needed no justification for its existence other than the fact that it was art, there was no incentive for the artist to produce works which evoked anything other than a pleasing esthetic response. Indeed, to have attempted to have done otherwise would have been to create something which, by definition, was inartistic.

The artist surrendered his social obligations, withdrew from society into a world of personal reverie, and produced art which either reflected his private fantasies or, more simply, his individual technical ingenuity.

If art was the only thing that mattered, it followed, therefore, that the artist would strive to make his creations as perfect as possible, for only by so doing could he hope for a measure of eternity. Thus Gautier, in stressing the relationship he felt should exist between literature and the plastic arts, demanded that the poet lavish his craftsman's skill on the achievement of perfect form and clarity of outline, just as a sculptor would carefully hew a figure from a block of marble. This theory he embodied in a collection of poems called *Emaux et Camées* (1853), the very title of which indicates the poet's intentions; and in the last poem of the 1857 edition of that volume be set forth his esthetic credo under the title "L'Art." Freely translated by Austin Dobson in 1876 as "Ars Victrix," the closing lines summarize the Parnassian position:

> All passes. ART alone
> Enduring stays to us;
> The bust outlasts the throne, —
> The Coin, Tiberius;
>
> Even the gods must go;
> Only the lofty Rhyme
> Not countless years o'erthrow, —
> Not long array of time.
>
> Paint, chisel, then, or write;
> but, that the word surpass,
> With the hard fashion fight, —
> With the resisting mass.

.Gautier's artfully chiseled lyrics with their sharply defined images inspired a group of writers who, calling themselves Parnassians, attempted to follow Gautier's precepts in their own verses. Among them was Théodore de Banville, whose *Petit traité de versification française* (1872) advocated the use of such old French forms as the *ballade, rondeau, triolet,* and the *virelay* and also stimulated a Parnassian movement in England. Austin Dobson, of course, whose *Proverbs in Porcelain* (1877) owed much to de Banville, was one of the poets involved; Andrew Lang's *Ballads in Blue China* (1872) is also indebted to de Banville; Edmund Gosse belonged to the group both by reason of his *Cornhill Magazine* article in July, 1872, entitled "A Plea for Certain Exotic Forms of Verse" (almost a résumé of de Banville's "*Petit traité*"), and on account of his poems which consistently followed Parnassian practice; and Lionel Johnson, also in the movement, contributed "A Note Upon the Practice and Theory of Verse at the Present Time Obtaining in France," to the *Century Guild Hobby Horse* in April, 1891, in which he contrasted the precise diction and well-defined images of the French with the admittedly grand but technically sloppy effects of much literature in England.[5]

Flecker should be set against this background of the Parnassian tradition, rather than against the Georgian; for almost from the beginning, he established himself as a careful, literary craftsman who devoted his skills to the composition of formal, precise, delicately structured lyrics and whose artificial style counted for more than content. Temperamentally, Flecker was cast for the role of a Georgian — no one gloried more in the delights of rural England than he — but in his verse, if one views his total achievement, one finds much less of the bucolic and rural than one might expect.

If one thinks of Flecker as a Parnassian, there is less danger of ascribing to his verse more intellectual depth and subtlety than is actually there. Flecker was above all "a craftsman in words";[6] and, though Herbert Howarth has suggested that Flecker (like T. S. Eliot), experienced new sensations but, unlike his more famous contemporary, was unable to find a new form in which to express them, one should not assume that Flecker was an especially significant figure in the history of the development of the modern esthetic.[7]

Flecker, unquestionably a serious poet, constantly revised his verses in an attempt to find le mot juste, the most harmonious combination of sounds, the perfectly poised meter; but he approached his verse more in the spirit of a meticulous line engraver than of an imaginative artist. As a child, he loved playing with Richter's stone architectural bricks,[8] a passion which outlasted boyhood; and he seems in his later years simply to have substituted words for stones. Flecker was more craftsman than prophet; a formal artist rather than a seer, he delighted in words more for their own sake than for the message they might communicate. Therefore, in surveying Flecker's poetical development, one should not expect to find much in the way of increasing intellectual maturity.

Certainly, as one would expect in the poetry of a man who was forced to recognize the prospect of an untimely death when he had hardly reached maturity, some of his last verses are more somber and introspective than those he wrote earlier. On the whole though, the substance of his poetry reveals comparatively little change; and, in so far as Flecker's poetic genius may be said to develop at all, it developed mainly in terms of his ability to manipulate his material rather than in his outlook on life. To put it bluntly, Flecker was a superficial person. He enjoyed life, but was not prone to introspection. He had his serious moments; but, one feels, these were not ones which prompted him to write his greatest poetry. The poet and the inner man rarely coincided, though they sometimes did; and, when they did so, Flecker produced verse of enduring quality.

II   The Bridge of Fire

The Bridge of Fire (1907), Flecker's first published collection of verse, established him as a somewhat late but representative poet of the fin de siècle. The volume is dedicated to his Oxford friend Jack Beazley, and Flecker evokes in the introduction his student days when he "rapturously trailed his gown" and gloried in the self-conscious artificiality of university life as he knew it then.[9] The contents recall much that is characteristic of the lesser poets of the decadent 1890s: the work of a clever undergraduate who slips easily into the appropriate role of a world-weary esthete, the poetry indicates he is bored with life and enamored with easeful death and langorous oblivion.

All the conventional ingredients are there: the stilted imagery; the tuneful melancholy; despair and ennui. There are femmes fatales such as Helen, "Slayer of Ships, Men, Cities"; Lucretia, "the strange woman, she the flower, the sword, /Red from spilt blood, a mortal flower to men, /Adorable, detestable";[10] and frail young men like Narcissus, "the sweet water boy more pallid/ Than any watery moon."[11] One can also detect echoes of Swinburne in "Lucretia," and perhaps of Oscar Wilde in "The Ballad of the Student in the South" who, like Dorian Gray, regards sin as a stage of experience in the search for wisdom.[12] Flecker's most obvious literary debt, however, is to Charles Baudelaire, the French poet who titillated fin-de-siècle undergraduate libidos and provoked the bourgeoisie to outbursts of moral indignation and to expressions of disgust. The presence of Baudelaire is most clearly seen in poems such as "Anapests," "The Litanies of Satan,"[13] and most noticeably of all in "The First Sonnet of Bathrolaire":

> Over the moonless land of Bathrolaire
> Rises at night, when revelry begins,
> A white unreal orb, a Sun that spins,
> And watches with a faint metallic stare
> The madly moving dance that they dance there,
> Whilst din and drone of ghostly violins
> Drown the triumphant shriek of obscene sins,
> And raise the incantation of despair.
> And all the spaces of that midnight Town
> Sound with appeal and sorrowful abuse.
> There some most lonely one: Some try to crown
> Mad lovers with sad boughs of formal yews,
> And Titan women wandering up and down
> Lead on the pale fanatics of the Muse.[14]

The Bridge of Fire also reveals Flecker's penchant for those two favorite flowers of the Decadents, lilies and roses. Lilies are especially profuse in "Mary Magdalen," a poem which begins with a line which might almost have been composed by Enoch Soames, the provincial Decadent poet of Max Beerbohm's satiric essay of the same name: "I have scarred the night with sin."[15] "Anapests" also contains lines which read like a parody of a typical Decadent lyric and, at the same time, aptly summarize Flecker's poetical preferences as revealed in his first volume of poems:

> Songs breathed to the tremulous ditties
> Of broken and harsh violins,
> Songs hinting the rose and the vine,
> Half drowned in the roar of red cities,
> And youthfully pleased at their sins,
> These songs I adore: they are mine.[16]

The Bridge of Fire also contains the first version of one of Flecker's best known poems, "Tenebris Interlucentem," and it is instructive to compare the early version with that which appeared in the *Collected Poems*. Such a comparison reveals how carefully the poet revised his work and also indicates the direction in which his poetic talents developed. Originally the poem read as follows:

> Once a poor songbird that had lost her way
> Sang down in Hell upon a blackened bough,
> Till all the lazy ghosts remembered how
> The forest trees stood up against the day.

> Then suddenly they knew that they had died,
> Hearing this music mock their shadow land:
> And some one there stole forth a timid hand
> To draw a phantom brother to his side.[17]

When "Tenebris Interlucentem" appeared in the *Collected Poems* it had been revised to read:

> A linnet who had lost her way
> Sang on a blackened bough in Hell,
> Till all the lazy ghosts remembered well
> The trees, the wind, the golden day.
>
> At last they knew that they had died
> When they heard music in that land,
> And some one there stole forth a hand
> To draw a brother to his side.[18]

In almost every way the second version is preferable to the earlier. In general, the slackness of the original poem has disappeared: superfluous epithets have been discarded; the imagery has been made more precise; the meter has been tightened. The result is that, whereas originally the poem had all the marks of being little more than an academic exercise, the later version has a note of genuine sadness, the more poignant when one recalls Flecker's fate. Instead of the vague "poor songbird," Flecker substitutes "linnet," which is preferable not simply because of its greater precision but also because it reinforces the idea of the bird as having lost its way, a linnet being the last creature one would expect to find in Hell. In the second line, the superfluous "down" has been suppressed; and the structure is inverted, thereby making the line conform more closely to normal grammatical usage, and also allowing the rhythmical stress to fall on the key words: "sang," "blackened," "bough," "Hell." In line three, the change from "how" to "well" intensifies the sense of loss experienced by the ghosts, as does the revised last line of the stanza, which more clearly evokes the "golden" sunlit world that they can no longer enjoy. In the first line of the second stanza, instead of the ghosts "suddenly" realizing that they are dead, they are made to know it "at last"; and there is a gain in subtlety — the incongruity of the bird's song dispels any doubts the ghosts may have had about their lifeless existence. In the following two lines, what was overly explicit is now muted; the unnecessary and self-consciously poetic "shadowy" disappears in favor of the more forceful "that"; and the gratuitous "timid" disappears altogether. From this comparative analysis, one can see the direction in which Flecker was working: toward greater economy, precision, and directness. His poetic development followed this pattern.

The Bridge of Fire should not be taken too seriously. The way the collection received its title is itself indicative of Flecker's attitude to the volume. One day, while he and Frank Savery were talking about the poems Flecker was gathering together for a collection, Flecker burst out: "I'll call it 'The Bridge of Fire,' and I'll write a poem with that name and put it in the middle of the book instead of at the beginning. That will be original and symbolic too." The more Flecker thought about it, the more he liked it. "It was a jolly good title," he said, "and he would easily be able to think of a poem to suit it."[19]

Neither should one take too seriously the persona Flecker adopts in *The Bridge of Fire*. "The lean and swarthy poet of despair," as he describes himself in "Envoy,"[20] is no more a description of Flecker's real personality than the pallor of "Narcissus" is a true indication of the poet's complexion. This difference Flecker himself took pains to emphasize after his collection had received an unflattering review from Douglas Goldring. "Our poets," wrote Goldring, "in too many cases have loved to pose as Pierrot babbling to the moon, smiling cynically to conceal a broken heart and unutterable desires; and Mr. Flecker . . . is no exception." To Goldring, Flecker's "factitious despair is a little absurd"; and, though willing to concede that, when the poet forgets to pose, "he is sometimes curiously effective," his general estimate of the *The Bridge of Fire* is rather low: "On the whole, Mr. Flecker's book has been something of a disappointment to us. He has a good ear, his verses are remarkably finished, and he is extremely accomplished; but he seems to have some defect of temperament which wars against his success, and to lack entirely that magic touch which gods often give (in their perversity) to quite dull and stupid people. It is a pity because he is very clever."[21]

This review prompted a reply from Flecker[22] in which he defended his verses by pointing out that they were, in effect, jeux d'esprit, referring to the doctrine of "art for art's sake" as justification for his poetical intentions. Goldring, who had drawn attention to the "unhealthy" character of Flecker's verses, classified Flecker as a typical exponent of the writing practiced by contributors to *The Yellow Book*, that notorious periodical of the 1890s which, not

altogether deservedly, has come to symbolize the spirit of fin de siècle. Flecker concentrates his attention on this aspect of Goldring's
review. "Art," he writes, echoing Oscar Wilde, "is good or bad; not
healthy or unhealthy; French or non-French; Yellow Book or non-
Yellow Book." Besides, he continues, "a love of pleasantly mal-
formed beasts," such as those which appear in the illustrations of
Aubrey Beardsley, onetime art editor of *The Yellow Book*, "seems
most delicately child-like and humorous." Therefore, "in such a fantastic mood it pleased me to call myself a sad comedian and most
tragic fool." Because Goldring had written that "the despair of Mr.
Flecker is rather absurd," Flecker replied, "better a tragic fool than
a dull fool. But can no one recognize any charm in a half-serious
rhetoric?" He continues: "Trammel rhetoric in verse, and its exaggeration, I thought, would appeal as at once sincere and
humorous. Of such outrageous and great humour in prose *Sartor
Resartus* is the example. I humbly wanted to try it in verse." In this
spirit, he said, he wrote his poem "The Oxford Canal" and
translated Baudelaire's "Litanies of Satan." Anyway, he asserts,
Baudelaire was far from being the "monstrous decadent" of popular
imagination. Instead, he was "an essentially classical poet, a master
of harmony and form . . . invariably careful to make his images cor-
respond to his sense"; and his poems were "the most virile poetic
productions of the nineteenth century in France." Finally,
emphasizing that as the poet of *The Bridge of Fire* he should not be
taken too seriously, he notes that, in so far as he has a personal
philosophy, it is of the conventional carpe diem kind, one perhaps
most clearly expressed in a poem about a wandering student:

> Darling, a scholar's fancies sink
> So faint beneath your song;
> And you are right, why should we think,
> We who are young and strong?
>
> We're of the people you and I,
> We do as others do;
> Linger and toil and laugh and die,
> And love the whole night through.

These carefree words, however, assume a more somber significance when one recalls Flecker's early death. In retrospect, as
Douglas Goldring has noted, Flecker seemingly had some premoni-

tion that he would not live long; therefore, he had to make every effort not to let one precious minute go to waste.[23] Unhappily, forced to live in uncongenial surroundings for several years, Flecker did let a number of those precious minutes go to waste; as his later volumes of verse indicate, much of his carefree attitude to life left him, and his factitious melancholy gave way to nostalgia and to genuine despair.

In *Thirty-Six Poems* (1910), Flecker's next volume of verse after *The Bridge of Fire*, a shift from Decadence to Estheticism occurs — from naughtiness and self-conscious ennui to a deliberate and almost single-minded concern for form and technique. No longer does the poet seem interested in shocking his readers; rather, he wishes to impress them with his artistry. The contents of this volume are almost entirely new, being either poems which Flecker had only recently written, or heavily revised versions of poems originally published in *The Bridge of Fire*. Only four pieces, "Riouperoux," "The Second Sonnet of Bathrolaire," "The Translator and the Children," and "The Destroyer of Ships, Men, Cities," remained unchanged from the earlier volume.

The poems which had been published in *The Bridge of Fire* and which reappear in revised form in *Thirty-Six Poems* are almost all changed for the better. Generally speaking, the more Decadent poems have been made less obviously fin de siècle; and a determined effort is made to achieve simplicity and economy: the lilies have been pruned in "Mary Magdalen"; the Devil has been banished from "Ideal," for the last line has been changed from "On Satan's horses will I ride" to the less energetic "On lunar seas my boat will glide."[24]

The two best poems in the collection are almost certainly "War Song of the Saracens,"[25] probably inspired by the Pre-Islamic Arab poet Antar's famous "If time would unmask its face"; and "The Town Without a Market"[26] which, as much as any poem in the volume, reflects Flecker's determined support of the "art-for-art's sake" ideal. Unlike his previous work in *The Bridge of Fire*, this poem depends on precisely observed detail rather than upon vaguely apprehended impressions. The opening lines, for example, establish the locale and communicate a clear description of the town:

> There lies afar behind a western hill
> The Town without a Market, white and still;

> For six feet long and not a third as high
> Are those small habitations.

From what follows, the reader learns that "the Town without a market" is in fact a cemetery; and the corpses, speaking through "tongueless teeth," recall the enjoyment of their existence before death and lament their fate. The poet, who says that all he had sought was peace, smiles "to hear them restless,"

> For I had not loved, I had not fought,
> And books are vanities, and manly strength
> A gathered flower.

His complacency is soon shattered, however, by the voice of a "timorous man, buried long years ago" who, it seems, was an artist, or at least a person of creative spirit, who says:

> On Earth I used to shape the Thing that seems,
> Master of all men, give me back my dreams.
> Give me that world that never failed me then,
> The hills I made and peopled with tall men,
> The palace that I built and called my home,
> My cities which could break the pride of Rome,
> The three queens hidden in the sacred tree,
> And those white cloud folk who sang to me.
> O Death, why hast thou covered me so deep?
> I was thy sister's child, the friend of Sleep.

And with this reminder that death robs man of everything, even of dreams, the poet retreats from his previous position; he realizes that "Death takes and cannot give," and so "Dark with no dream is hateful." Life is after all preferable. All man's activities and achievements are vain and destined to perish; but this fact is no reason to seek death. On the contrary, because man has been granted the capacity to dream, in effect to create, life is to be enjoyed because only in life can one's creative impulses find expression.

In the poem "To a Poet a Thousand Years Hence," Flecker again affirms his belief in the importance of art, the one activity of man which has an enduring quality. In this instance, however, he, taking a more positive view, implies that the poet's work lives on after death. How else may man conquer, if not through art? Therefore,

O friend unseen, unborn, unknown,
Student of our sweet English tongue,
Read out my words at night, alone:
I was a poet; I was young.

Since I can never see your face,
And never shake you by the hand,
I send my soul through time and space
To greet you. You will understand.[27]

A touch of A. E. Housman is perhaps present in this poem, but the academic game of hunt the influence, if played too intensely, can sometimes end with the participants' making fools of themselves. In this instance, however, although it is next to impossible to say which particular poem of Housman "To a Poet a Thousand Years Hence" reminds one of, one can say that the spare, unadorned diction and the wryly reflective tone are reminiscent of Flecker's slightly older contemporary. One also knows that, when *Thirty-Six Poems* was being written, Flecker was an admirer of Housman. In an essay written while Flecker was at Cambridge, he had said that "of all volumes of modern verse *The Shropshire Lad* is the most complete indication of this new and simple style,"[28] and more than likely Flecker studied the poet whose style embodied so much of what he was trying at this time to achieve.

John Davidson also appears to have left his mark on the contents of *Thirty-Six Poems.* In an essay about Davidson, also written at this time,[29] Flecker places special emphasis on the poet's "realism," which he found a healthy antidote to "our quiet self-satisfied, ill-founded idealism"; and one can state with some confidence that two Flecker poems at least, "The Ballad of the Londoner" and "The Ballad of Camden Town,"[30] both of which are notable for their "realism," are strongly reminiscent of the Scottish poet in both form and social attitude.

III The Golden Journey to Samarkand

Thirty-Six Poems was published by the Adelphi Press, but the publisher ran into difficulties shortly afterwards and was forced out of business. Accordingly, Flecker was obliged to approach another publisher, J. M. Dent; and in 1911 this publisher reissued the volume, plus six more poems which Flecker had written in the meantime. The collection was entitled simply, if predictably, *Forty-Two*

Poems.[31] The bulk of these verses had either been written or extensively revised while Flecker was at Cambridge; during this period he
had been an earnest Parnassian and that influence is clearly
traceable in a number of poems.

In Flecker's next volume of verse, *The Golden Journey to
Samarkand* (1913), his most distinguished one, the Parnassian influence is paramount; and the poet openly declares in an introduction to this collection his Parnassian allegiances.[32] There is little in
his brief prefatory essay which one could consider novel since the
content is similar to Leconte de Lîsle's preface to *Poèmes Antiques*
(1852). Flecker states simply that all he can do is praise a very simple
theory of poetry "which has a great attraction for him," that of "the
French Parnasse." He asserts that he does not necessarily believe
that the best poetry in the world is Parnassian; but, because poetic
criticism and poetry in England are at the present time in a chaotic
state, a program such as that proposed by the Parnassians could have
a salutary effect in restoring order. "No worthless writer will be
redeemed by the excellence of the poetic theory he may chance to
hold," but "a sound theory can produce sound practice, and exercise
a beneficent effect on writers of genius" as "has been repeatedly
proved in the short but glorious history of 'the Parnasse'."

Acknowledging the difficulty of describing what the term "Parnassian" means, Flecker states that one may perhaps arrive at a
suitable definition by considering first what "Parnassian" is not: "To
be didactic like Wordsworth, to write dull poems of unwieldy length,
to bury, like Tennyson or Browning, poetry of exquisite beauty in
monstrous realms of vulgar, feeble, or obscure versifying, to overlay
fine work with gross and irrelevant egoism, like Victor Hugo, would
be abhorrent, and rightly so, to members of this school." Considering some of the specific charactristic features of the movement,
he notes the tendency of the Parnassians to use traditional forms,
and even to employ classical subjects. Above all, he says, the Parnassian's desire in writing poetry is "to create beauty: his inclination
is toward a beauty somewhat statuesque. He is apt to be dramatic
and objective rather than intimate." Some people, he concedes, have
found this kind of poetry "frigid and unemotional"; but in reply to
this criticism one can only advise, "Read the verse of Hérédia,
Leconte de Lîsle, Samain, Henri de Régnier and Jean Moréas."

It is apparent, however, that Flecker is less bound by the specifics
of the Parnassian program than one might imagine. The main reason
for his declaring his allegiance to the school, it seems, is his belief

that English poetry "stands in need of some such saving doctrine to redeem it from formlessness and didacticism, especially the latter." If the poet must preach, he should write his sermons in prose: "It is not the poet's business to save man's soul, but to make it worth saving." Great poetry can only be judged in terms of "art for art's sake"; and by that Flecker means art in the broadest sense in so far as it embraces "all life and all humanity, and sees, in the temporary and fleeting doctrines of conservative or revolutionary, only the human grandeur or passion that inspires them." Therefore, he concludes, his main intention in *The Golden Journey to Samarkand* is not to edify but to create beauty, and only in accordance with this principle should he be judged.[33]

Like much that Flecker wrote, however, one should not take this preface too seriously. In a letter of December 15, 1913, to Geraldine Hodgson, Flecker warned his correspondent that, though the preface was "absolutely sincere," it was, nonetheless, "a wicked piece of work." Then, clarifying his enigmatic remark, he wrote: "It was no good just writing poetry and flinging it at the public's head — especially if your poetry isn't all of one piece, but rather apt to vary with moods. If one wrote *only* Oriental poems, for instance, the critics would say, This follower of Fitzgerald etc. etc. So I had to give myself a label. I had to proclaim a *message*. Of course it succeeded. I have irritated some and pleased others — but now I am labelled." Nevertheless, he continues,

The Preface, as I say, is quite sincere, and I'm glad you took it as such. But, of course, one can't compress into a few pages all one has to say on so vast a subject. For instance, one might imagine that by cursing the men with a message, I was cursing some people that don't exist. But the message nowadays is usually an 'immoral one,' a revolutionary one. It is the art of Ibsen, of Shaw, of Galsworthy, the whole of modern drama at its best; it is Swinburne, Shelley, Browning at their worst who have been ruined. It is not so simple to say what I mean. The message gives the enthusiasm: the enthusiasm is a glorious thing: Shelley is a greater poet than Leconte de Lîsle or Hérédia because of his enthusiasm for a lot of very dull doctrines of Godwin's. No Parnassian ever rose to the height of *Hellas*. No Parnassian ever fell as low as *Peter Bell*. Shelley's enthusiasms made a flame of his poetry: Swinburne's obsessed him till they burnt up his genius by killing his sense of proportion. He forgot to interest himself in words, or new impressions: as long as there was liberty, and the sea, and the big metre, and a few of his old stock epithets, he thought he could go on renewing for ever the inspiration of *Dolores*.

Then, turning to attack John Masefield, whose iconoclastic *Salt Water Ballads* (1902) and the spate of poems which followed caught the popular imagination with their slangy realism and breezy rhythms, Flecker continues:

But the sin I hate in Masefield, whose genius I once admired, is a quite different and more subtle variety of the message. He has no message whatever, but it struck him that the public wanted one. He didn't directly preach. But he infected his long poems with a sham manliness, a sham religiosity, a sham roughness. He seems to stand away from his poem and shout at one like a travelling showman. Please observe. See how modern my hero is. How bravely he swears. How manly he is. How religiously he dies. Observe, I go down into the slums for my hero; how new and noble that is of me. Masefield's remedy.

In other words, Flecker concludes, "the narrowing of poetry comes from the preachers." However odd it may seem, Shakespeare was the great Parnassian, "for he was interested in man, not in any narrowing theories of man. It is Paul Fort," one of the later French Parnassians, "who can show us what it is to be a Poet; it simply means an enthusiasm for the world in every detail."[34]

Although one or two poems in *The Golden Journey to Samarkand* may be said to have a "message" — to invite the reader to ponder certain basic questions relevant to man's existence as in the poem from which the volume derives its title[35] — most of them seem to have been written in an attempt to create "beauty." One of the best and most typical poems in the collection is "A Ship, an Isle, a Sickle Moon":

> A ship, an isle, a sickle moon —
> With few but with how splendid stars
> The mirrors of the sea are strewn
> Between their silver bars!
>
> An isle beside an isle she lay,
> The pale ship anchored in the bay,
> While in the young moon's port of gold
> A star-ship — as the mirrors told —
> Put forth its great and lonely light
> To the unreflecting Ocean, Night.
> And still, a ship upon her seas,
> The isle and the island cypresses

Went sailing on without the gale:
And still there moved the moon so pale,
A crescent ship without a sail![36]

All the conventional Parnassian ingredients are present: the coolly
observed detail; the metallic imagery; the immobility of the scene
the poet describes; the rigid attention to form. But this poem is more
than an exercise in Parnassianism; for as Flecker himself observed,
there is more in the poem than appears at first reading. As he said, it
is a "very subtle" composition, one which would appear more so if
one were familiar with Henri de Régnier.[37] It is, in short, a symbolic
poem, the meaning of which is rather obscure; but familiarity with
de Régnier's writings helps to clarify Flecker's intentions.

Henri de Régnier (1864-1936), French poet and novelist, studied,
like Flecker, for the diplomatic service; but, as his family was better
able financially to support a would-be writer, he was able to abandon
his prospective career as a civil servant and devote his attention to
literature. He soon became well known in French Symbolist circles,
achieving a measure of literary fame for his successful handling of
the free verse form, which he employed in a great many poems included in *Poèmes anciens et Romanesques* (1890), *Tel qu'en songe*
(1892), and *Jeux rustiques et divins* (1897), his most notable early
collections of verse. In his later years, he tended to concentrate more
and more on Classical subjects and forms; his interest in free verse
became less apparent as time went on; and he finally devoted most
of his energy to writing precious, self-consciously ornate novels set in
the seventeenth and eighteenth centuries.

Apart from de Régnier's interest in Parnassian techniques, Flecker
was probably drawn to the poet on account of a basic similarity of
temperament. Like Flecker, de Régnier was also a dreamer who es-
caped from a world which never quite lived up to his expectations
into an exotic environment where all was colorful enchantment. De
Régnier lost himself in the Classical world of Greece; Flecker sought
his escape also in Greece, as well as in the Orient of Sir Richard Burton's *Arabian Nights*. But de Régnier, cushioned from reality by the
comforts conferred upon him by his affluence, experienced no disillusionment: Hellenistic Greece remained for him a secure haven,
and his spirit was able to develop under its influence. Flecker, forced
by the exigencies of his financial situation to earn his living in the
East, soon found that his vision of the Orient was far removed from

actuality; the dream became a nightmare, and he spent the greater part of his energies trying to escape from an environment which he found increasingly intolerable.

Thus, what Flecker may have meant when he told Frank Savery that de Règnier held the key to "A Ship, an Isle, a Sickle Moon" was that the poem gave symbolic expression to his sense of disillusionment. The ship appears to symbolize Flecker's attempts to recreate his romantic visions — his poetry, perhaps, by which Flecker sought to reach his island dream world. At first, all seems well, for the ship and the isle seem to be compatible: "An isle beside an isle she lay, /The pale ship anchored in the bay." But then another vessel, "a star-ship appears, "putting forth its great and lonely light" — reality, truth, perhaps? — and, though the first ship and "the isle and island cypresses" all go "sailing on," they are mocked by "the star-ship, the moon so pale" which "moves on without a sail." In other words, the dream and Flecker's re-creation of it, have a beautiful existence of their own; but, meanwhile, truth, inaccessible and remote, lies beyond the reach of the poet and his dreams.

That this interpretation of Flecker's poem is close to what the poet intended to communicate is supported by another poem in the same volume, "Oak and Olive," which follows immediately after "A Ship, an Isle, a Sickle Moon." In this poem, Flecker gives a more explicit expression of his inability to realize his dreams; and he acknowledges the tremendous hold England has on his imagination, one which inhibited him in his attempt to establish close ties with his exotic vision. "Oak and Olive," one of Flecker's best poems, is certainly one of his most honest; and it is vital for a proper understanding of the emotional conflict which conditioned the poet's personality:

I

Though I was born a Londoner,
And bred in Gloucestershire,
I walked in Hellas years ago
With friends in white attire:
And I remember how my soul
Drank wine as pure as fire.

And when I stand by Charing Cross
I can forget to hear
The crash of all those smoking wheels,
When those cold flutes and clear

Pipe with such fury down the street,
My hands grow moist with fear.

And there's a hall in Bloomsbury
No more I dare to tread,
For all the stone men shout at me
And swear they are not dead;
And once I touched a broken girl
And knew that marble bled.

II

But when I walk in Athens town
That swims in dust and sun
Perverse, I think of London then,
Where massive work is done,
And with what sweep at Westminster
The rayless waters run.

I ponder how from Attic seed
There grew an English tree,
How Byron like his heroes fell,
Fighting a country free,
And Swinburne took from Shelley's lips
The kiss of Poetry.

And while our poets chanted Pan
Back to his pipes and power,
Great Verral, bending at his desk,
And searching hour on hour
Found out old gardens, where the wise
May pluck a Spartan flower.

III

When I go down the Gloucester lanes
My friends are deaf and blind:
Fast as they turn their foolish eyes
The Macnads leap behind,
And when I hear the fire-winged feet,
They only hear the wind.

Have I not chased the fluting Pan
Through Cranham's sober trees?
Have I not sat on Painswick Hill

With a nymph upon my knees,
And she as rosy as the dawn
And naked as the breeze?

IV

But when I lie in Grecian fields,
Smothered in asphodel,
Or climb the blue and barren hills,
Or sing in woods that smell
With such hot spices of the South
As mariners might sell —

Then my heart turns where no sun burns,
To lands of glittering rain,
To fields beneath low clouded skies
New-widowed of their grain,
And autumn leaves like blood and gold
That strew a Gloucester lane.

V

Oh well I know sweet Hellas now,
And well I knew it then,
When I with starry lads walked out —
But ah, for home again!
Was I not bred in Gloucestershire
One of the Englishmen![38]

It is odd to think that Flecker wrote these verses at the time of his engagement to Hellé Skiardaressi, and even his insistence that the poem is "a jest after all in the good old manner" cannot take away the unpleasant taste.[39] Flecker could be remarkably tactless where other people's feelings were concerned. Can it be that the closing stanza contains a direct reference to his fiancée (well I know sweet Hellas now")? If so, she must have been a remarkably stupid or exceptionally understanding woman not to have been deeply upset; for Flecker seems to be saying that a closer familiarity with Greece has simply reinforced his nostalgia for England. What the poem does make clear, however, is Flecker's ambivalent feeling about the exotic: he was strongly fascinated by it, but he was unable to relinquish his English identity and merge with it.

As both "A Ship, an Isle, a Sickle Moon" and "Oak and Olive" demonstrate, Flecker had moved beyond the imagism and formal preoccupations of the Parnassians; he had entered the world of the Symbolists. It is difficult to summarize the Symbolists' aims because, unlike the Parnassians, they had no clearly defined program. Briefly, one may state that the Symbolists were rebelling against prevailing literary conventions — in France, where the movement was most significant, this meant the explicit moralizing and vapid romanticism of Victor Hugo and Alfred de Vigny. During the early part of the nineteenth century, science, which had made rapid advances, had reduced the miraculous to the commonplace; and it had made man appear as an insignificant unit in the grand complexity of the universe.

The Symbolists, conscious of man's decreasing stature, attempted to give the individual a sense of identity and status by focusing attention on his personal thoughts and feelings. In terms of the visual arts, the theatrical grandeur of Eugene Delacroix gave way to the muted suggestiveness of Edouard Manet; in literature, the sweeping idealism of Victor Hugo's belief in mankind was replaced by the personal impressions of Stéphane Mallarmé. In order to communicate this new vision, the Symbolists abandoned explicit generalization and abstraction; they attempted to render faithfully man's individual sensations, thoughts, and feelings by using a new idiom — one evocative rather than explicit, suggestive rather than dogmatic. The brief direct statement was abandoned in favor of symbolism.[40]

The poets most closely associated with the Symbolist movement in France were Villiers de l'Isle Adam, Arthur Rimbaud, Paul Verlaine, and Stéphane Mallarmé, and such less familiar figures as Henri de Régnier, Albert Samain, Jean Moréas, and Paul Fort; and the work of the last four, especially, was well known to Flecker. Curiously, Flecker's poetry reveals little influence from the better known writers, but several of his best poems owe much to the work of the latter group. "The Gates of Damascus," for example, which he referred to in a letter to Frank Savery of July, 1913, as his best poem,[41] is clearly related to de Régnier's "Pour les Portes des Guerriers," which Flecker also translated,[42] as well as to the same poet's "Pour la Porte sur la Mer" and "Pour la Porte' des Marchands," both of which were included in de Régnier's *Inscriptions*. Flecker's poem was also influenced by a visit he and his wife made late in 1911 to the "Bawabat Allah" in Damascus.[43]

The poem[44] begins with the information that Damascus has four gates, each of which has a warden who sings a song explaining the symbolic properties of the entrance he has been appointed to guard. The East Gate, looking toward Iraq, is "the Postern of Fate, the Desert Gate, Disaster's Cavern, Fort of Fear"; and the warden cautions those who pass through it that the way ahead is fraught with danger and death. The West Gate, looking toward the sea, gives promise of a less perilous journey; but, though the way may be easier, the dangers are nonetheless there, for in "utmost West" King Solomon sits, gripping his magic ring: "And when that ring is stolen, he will rise in outraged majesty, And take the World upon his back, and fling the World beyond the sea."

The North Gate's warden, "who singeth fast, but drinketh faster," guards the gate to Aleppo; and, though a journey in this direction is not in the least hazardous, there are, nonetheless, dangers of a different kind, to the soul at least, for this is the way that the traders who sell "the rotten" and buy "the ripe" travel. The Gate to the South, "the arch of Allah," is the gate through which the pilgrims to Mecca travel; and the warden prays that those who pass through will receive God's blessing because, at the end of their journey, they may learn "who walks thy garden eve on eve, and bows his head, and calls thee Friend."

The meaning of the poem is clear enough. Those who elect to pursue the way of agressive confrontation with danger, those who seek sensual pleasures, and those who seek material wealth are tempting Fate. Only those who yearn for a transcendental reality are following the proper course, for knowledge of God alone can set the soul at rest. That Flecker, who delighted in a purely physical existence, should seek to eulogize the glory of God and the pleasures of the soul is unusual. It may be, of course, that the subject of the Gates of Damascus appealed to him simply as a means of creating "beauty," as a way of demonstrating his poetic talent. On the other hand, it may be that Flecker, now forced to face the possibility of an early death, had become more attracted to mysticism. It may be that this poem is an expression of genuine belief. Certainly, other poems that Flecker wrote at this time support the view that, during the last year or so of his life, he was frequently less occupied with this world than with the next.

In "The Dying Patriot," for example, another Symbolist poem, (one later included in his play *Don Juan*), Flecker describes a patriot's dying thoughts as he recalls England's past as well as her imperialist obligations of the present:

Day breaks on England down the Kentish hills,
Singing in the silence of the meadow-footing rills,
Day of my dreams, O day!
    I saw them march from Dover, long ago,
    With a silver cross before them, singing low,
Monks of Rome from their home where the blue seas break in foam,
Augustine with his feet of snow.

Noon strikes on England, noon on Oxford town,
— Beauty she was statue cold — there's blood upon her gown:
Noon of my dreams, O noon!
    Proud and godly kings had built her, long ago,
    With her towers and tombs and statues all arow,
With her fair and floral air and the love that lingers there,
And the streets where the great men go.

Evening on the olden, the golden sea of Wales,
When the first star shivers and the last wave pales:
O evening dreams!
    There's a house that Britons walked in, long ago,
    Where now the springs of ocean fall and flow,
And the dead robed in red and sea-lilies overhead
    Sway when the long winds blow.

Sleep not, my country: though night is here, afar
Your children of the morning are clamorous for war:
    Fire in the night, O dreams!
    Though she send you as she sent you, long ago,
    South to desert, east to ocean, west to snow,
West of these out to seas colder than the Hebrides I must go
Where the fleet of stars is anchored and the young Star-captains glow.[45]

Although the general drift of this poem is clear enough, it is obscure in many of its details. Fortunately, in a letter of November 23, 1911, to T. M. A. Cooper, a teacher at Dean Close School with whom Flecker corresponded intermittently for a number of years, he elucidates:

The patriot has been shot: and as he dies, very *mistily* he thinks of England from East to West — Dover suggests Augustine to him — its most important connexion with English history. Oxford is in the middle of England, and he mixes it madly with the sun voyaging over England — and the blood is suggested by his own blood and is a piece of mental wandering, quite in keeping dramatically, but I admit puzzling out of its context.

Floral air — is after all a very ordinary expression for sweet or flower-scented air, and you can smell it in the Lime Walk of Trinity Quad any spring day.

Feet of snow — I'd forgotten; just symbolic of the purity of Augustine's fervour — and mind you he was probably barefoot.

Surely you know the legend of the drowned lands off Wales — or rather the fact that large parts of Carnarvon Bay were submerged. The patriot is dying in London at night, and he thinks of the parts of the Empire that are in sunrise. The chill of death suggests to his wandering fancies the Hebrides and the cold seas; for you see the poem is dramatic and not lyrical.[46]

In spite of Flecker's clarification, "The Dying Patriot" remains an unsatisfactory poem; it is clever, perhaps, but not especially moving or sincere. It is interesting, however, as an example of Flecker's increasing interest in Symbolism; and its melancholy subject is characteristic of much of the verse he wrote at this time, as, for example, "Brumana" and "In Hospital."[47] "In Hospital," like "The Gates of Damascus," also reveals Flecker's growing interest in the possibility of a transcendental state after death.

In Switzerland, Flecker became an enthusiastic admirer of Paul Fort (1871-1960), the so-called "Prince of Poets," who is best known, perhaps, as the founder and editor of the journal *Vers et Prose* with which Paul Valéry became closely associated. Flecker found Fort's work in the library at Leysin, and he immediately wrote to Frank Savery announcing his discovery of "perhaps the greatest of all French poets."[48] He also wrote an appreciative essay about Fort for the *Nineteenth Century Review*,[49] in which he made it clear why he was so impressed by his writing, and from his account one may see that Flecker believed he had found in Fort a truly kindred soul.

Flecker admires Fort's "gaiety and imagination," and he draws attention to the poet's deep and sensitive appreciation of the French countryside. Fort's most "obvious and pervading" characteristic, however, is his humor — a humor "which combines with an impudence almost English a lightness entirely French" — a quality which makes his "paganism" attractive and saves it from the "factitious manliness" which many English writers use "to palliate anything which a very timorous curate might find shocking." As for Fort's philosophy, he believes that "the divine function . . . is to dream for dream or imagination is a creative force. There is no creative vision in stone, but everything that is alive has a certain power of vision and is therefore, God." It follows, therefore, that the poet, "who above other men possesses the faculty of creative imagination, is the greatest god on earth." It is true, continues Flecker, who reveals how firm his allegiance was to the Parnassian school, that Fort's poetry is frequently marred by careless craftsmanship which comes about as a result of his thinking in verses rather than in lines of poetry. Sometimes his verse degenerates into mere prose; but, he concludes, Fort in spirit is so close to the Shakespeare of *Midsummer Night's Dream* that he is one of the few French poets who should be "profoundly appreciated by English readers."

One can understand why Flecker should have been so appreciative of Paul Fort, especially since he provided a convenient philosophical justification for dreaming, thereby transforming Flecker's escapist reveries into the proper function of the true poet. It is understandable, too, that many of Flecker's last poems reflect Fort's sentiments and ideas. In "Philomel," a direct translation of Fort's poem from the French, Flecker exhorts the reader to "turn down to Earth and hear . . . the noise of a great Heart upon the grass."[50] "The Pensive Prisoner," "Hexameters," 'Blue Noon," and "Stillness" — all of which have for their theme the desirability of moving into a transcendental state by way of an imaginative appreciation of the physical world — also reveal Fort's influence.[51] "Blue Noon" expresses this idea most clearly; but "Stillness," described by an anonymous reviewer in *The Times Literary Supplement* as Flecker's best poem,[52] is a more personal statement of Fort's philosophy, and it also evokes Flecker's own career and imminent death:

> When the words rustle no more,
>   And the last work is done,
> When the bolt lies deep in the door,
>   And Fire, our Sun,
> Falls on the dark-laned meadows of the Floor;
>
> When from the clock's last chime to the next chime
>   Silence beats his drum,
> And Space with gaunt grey eyes and her brother Time
>   Wheeling and whispering come,
> She with the mould of form and he with the loom of rhyme:
>
> Then twittering out in the night my thought-birds flee,
>   I am emptied of all my dreams:

I only hear Earth turning, only see
     Ether's long bankless streams,
And only know I should drown if you laid not your hand on me.

It would be mistaken romanticism to assume that, during Flecker's last months, the poet of the senses became the poet of the spirit. There is, certainly, an increasing tendency toward introspection and mysticism in his last poetry; but Flecker remained to the end the poetic craftsman, who wrote less as a means of communicating his innermost thoughts and feelings than for the sheer joy of manipulating words and creating subtle, complex rhythms. For Flecker, poetry was as much an intellectual exercise as a means of expression; and, though many of his last poems have personal implications, Flecker was primarily a "maker," an "articulator of sweet sounds together," to borrow W. B. Yeats's phrase. Poetry appealed to Flecker largely — to quote Yeats again — because of "the fascination of what's difficult."

In this spirit, Flecker, shortly before his death, set himself the task of translating Virgil's *Aeneid* in quantitative hexameters; and he was inspired by William Johnson Stone's essay "On Classical Metres in English Verse," which prefaced Robert Bridges' *Milton's Prosody* (1901).[53] Before he died, Flecker managed to complete some lines, specifically the episode of the descent of Aeneas, under Hecate's guidance, to Avernus in Book VI. Flecker's translation is fluent without being facile, stately without being pompous:

They went obscure in lowering lone night
Through lodges of King Dis, untenanted, —
Featureless lands. Thus goes a forest pathway
Beneath the curst light of the wav'ring moon,
When Jove has gloomed the sky, and pitchy dark
Uncoloured all the world. In Hell's first reach
Fronting the very vestibule of Orcus
Griefs and the Cares have set their couches down, —
The vengeful Cares. There pale diseases dwell,
Sad Eld and Fear and loathesome Poverty
And Hunger, that bad counsellor — dire shapes —
And Death and Toil, and Sleep brother of Death
And soul-corrupting joys.

Occasionally, he falls for the banal poeticism — "domain," "eld," "marge" — but such examples are few. He also sometimes translates

the Latin almost word for word and ignores the necessity of transforming the syntax as well as the vocabulary:

> The Priestess,
> Seeing his dragon necks stiffen to strike,
> A cake of honey and bemusing herbs
> Tossed him.

On the whole, however, his translation is of sufficiently high quality
to make one wish he had had time to do more.[54]
    Translating Virgil must have been a welcome escape from the
pains of the sickbed and from the pressing clamor of the war, but
Flecker also attempted on more than one occasion to write poetry
which reflected contemporary events. Unhappily, he was unable to
transcend in his war poems the patriotic stoicism of Rudyard Kipling
and Julian Grenfell; and his piece "The Burial in England,"[55]
though it has some of the measured stateliness of his *Aeneid* translation, is sober but undistinguished. "God Save the King," even in its
revised and improved version, hovers between the commonplace
and the banal.[56] Among these very last poems, however, one piece
stands out; it is not sufficiently good to be included among his best
work, but it is competent enough; and it is also arresting because it
reflects characteristics of his personality. In "The True Paradise,"
the poet, looking toward death, yearns for a heaven that will remind
him of home; he beseeches God to grant him "earth's treats in
paradise." He wishes for a world remade "less Man's and Nature's
Pain,"

> So I and all my friends, still young, still wise,
> Will shout along thy streets 'O Paradise!'
> But if prepared for me new Mansions are,
> Chill and unknown, in some bright windy star,
> Mid Strange-shaped Souls from all the Planets seven,
> Lord, I fear deep, and would not go to Heaven.
> Rather in feather-mist I'd fade away
> Like the Dawn-writing of an April day.[57]

Flecker's was not a tough spirit. There is little stoicism in his
verse; and, when it is there, as it is in "The Burial in England," it is
hollow, factitious. A dreamer to the end, he yearned for a world
without pain; but he was unable, or not caring, to transform his
dreams into visions. Toward the end, his sensuous escapism was

tempered with thoughts of death and with what lay beyond; but, unlike Keats, who also died of consumption and whose poetic career is
somewhat similar to Flecker's, he was never able to universalize his
emotions. Flecker saw the world from his own, individual perspective. Prone to selfishness throughout his life, he did not change when
confronted with death.

CHAPTER 4

The Prose

I *Literary Criticism*

FLECKER'S prose is more interesting for the light it throws on his personality and on his poetry and drama that it is in itself. It consists of critical essays, travel sketches, a textbook for students of Italian, some visionary fantasies, translations, a dialogue on education, and a romantic novel, *The King of Alsander*. Most of this work is not especially significant, and the novel must be considered a failure. Among the critical essays included in the *Collected Prose* are two on John Davidson; others on A. E. Housman, W. J. Courthope and Arthur Symons, Paul Fort, "The Public as Art Critic"; and one which amounts to a critical evaluation of the Parnassians, being the preface to *The Golden Journey to Samarkand*. Though not distinguished, none of these essays is of poor quality; and the earlier ones are quite remarkable if one considers Flecker's youthfulness when he wrote them.

The earlier of the Davidson pieces, for example, "John Davidson: Realist,"[1] was written while Flecker was still an undergraduate at Oxford. It is an enthusiastic encomium to a poet who, wrote Flecker, provided "an antidote to our quiet, self-satisfied, ill founded idealism"; and, though inclined to overpraise him and to elevate the stature of works which most readers would be inclined to ignore, Flecker does make clear why Davidson appealed to him and puts forward a plausible case in support of him. Davidson was an iconoclast, a man who wished to sweep away hypocrisy and humbug; and these anarchic tendencies recommended themselves to Flecker, who at the time the essay was written was rebelling against the restrictive influence of his pious, morally conventional home. Davidson, claims Flecker, had gone even farther in breaking conventions than Ibsen: Ibsen "urged the overhauling of all our social machinery; he attacked with terrible precision the shoddy idealism

and the prudish self-complacency that still pervades modern life";
Davidson, however, urges one "to live as if convention, as if
Christianity, as if thirty centuries of literature had never existed."

In "John Davidson,"[2] Flecker's later critical estimate of the poet,
he is more temperate and does not allow his enthusiasm for the man
to influence his judgment of the work. Previously, he had praised
Davidson's turgid farce *Smith*, with which, Flecker had said,
"something vital" came into English literature; and he had had also
much admiration for the long, blank-verse "testaments." Now,
however, Flecker, who has Davidson's literary achievements more
clearly in perspective, admits that, though Davidson was certainly
the greatest poet of his age, his was not an especially glorious age.
He selects for special mention Davidson's ballads, and he now
denigrates the testaments — critical judgments with which most
modern readers would agree. Finally, in seeking an explanation for
Davidson's comparative failure as a poet, Flecker states that, though
he was a man of genius, he was also a man of great ambition; and
"his ambition ruined his genius" by causing him to become asser-
tive, shrill, and rather vulgar.

The Davidson essays tell more about Flecker's rebellious tendencies than about his literary taste, but an unfinished piece entitled
"The New Poetry and Mr. A. E. Housman's 'Shropshire Lad',"[3]
written while Flecker was at Cambridge, gives insight into Flecker's
criteria for poetic excellence and, incidentally, makes a series of
critical judgments with which most modern readers would agree. He
observes that many people are ready to insist that poetry is dead, but
what they really mean is that the "older poetry," that "splendid con-
nected dynasty" from Coleridge to Swinburne, is dead. But, he continues, this is no real cause for regret because, in estimating the
worth of poetry written in the "old" tradition, one is apt to confuse
grandeur with worth, noble sentiments with poetic ability — a confusion which has led some people to overestimate the value of this
kind of writing, particularly with respect to such modern followers of
the old tradition as Stephen Phillips and William Watson. What
Flecker admires is simplicity, the spare, clear diction of parts of
Oscar Wilde's "Ballad of Reading Gaol"; he likes also the
characteristic language of the verse of Robert Bridges, Thomas Hardy, W. B. Yeats, and, most notably, A. E. Housman, who uses "pure
spoken English with hardly any admixture of poetic verbiage."

In another essay, "Two Critics of Poetry,"[4] Flecker praises Arthur
Symons at the expense of W. J. Courthope. Courthope, writes
Flecker, estimates poets by their "influence" rather than by their

"merit"; and, since he has an evident enthusiasm for "verse which he considers patriotic and healthy," he dismissed Keats and Blake as "conceited asses with a spark of genius" because neither of them, he says, were much interested in politics and society. Symons, on the other hand, who "prefers poetry to politics," is good on the Romantic poets; he is inclined to underestimate Alexander Pope and his contemporaries; but he is,writes Flecker, a much sounder critic than Courthope. According to Flecker, Symons is the better critic because he focuses attention on the poetry and arrives at his judgments on the basis of a clear-sighted, sensitive appraisal of the words the poet has written. Symons considers poetry as poetry, not merely as a means of expressing something which might perhaps be better expressed in prose.

With the exception of the earlier Davidson essay, the idea that poetry should be criticized simply as poetry is a theme which runs throughout Flecker's literary criticism, but it is expressed most forcefully in "The Public as Art Critic"[5] in which he enumerates the qualities that the perfect critic should have. He should know all about the technical aspects of writing verse, but he should avoid being pedantic about them. Most important of all, he should have "a deep experience of life," that will enable him to judge without puritanism and prejudice:

He must not condemn poems because they are morbid, profane, or deal with what the Manchester Watch Committee . . . would call unpleasant subjects. He will know that art is divided, not into decadent and healthy, classic and romantic, but into the two mighty divisions of Good and Bad, and that these divisions alone hold true. One great dogma alone he must hold — that human life is passionately interesting in all its phases, that over the filthiest by-ways the sky of night must stretch its flowery mantle of stars. The critic must be of purer mould than the poet himself. He must have a profound love for man, not the vague enthusiasm of the humanitarian, but a vivid delight in all the men in the world, men sinful, men splendid, men coarse, or cowardly, or pathetic. And in all the phenomena of nature, sordid or shining, the background to our tragedy, he must admire, if not the beauty, then the force, the law, the cruelty, and the power. And with this enthusiasm in his soul he will bitterly condemn dullness, weakness, bad workmanship, vulgar thought, shoddy sentiment as being slanders on mankind; and in this sense and this sense only — that is the glory of man — great art is moral.[6]

Finally, conscious that he may have created an impossible ideal against which few critics could measure themselves, Flecker carefully indicates that he is not saying that art is only for the elect.

On the contrary, there is the "spark of the divine in us all";
therefore, it is quite possible that "thousands honestly and genuinely
enjoy, admire, and love certain works of art which they know to be
considered great." Nevertheless, in spite of this concession to the
masses, Flecker really does believe that the public is, by and large,
philistine. Art lives on, it is true, but in noble retirement:

The artist hears all around him infinite rubbish talked about his art, and imagines for the moment that the middle classes are sincere, and will be willing
at least to hear his symphony or read his book. You soon undeceive him, you
middle classes. You, who have let, are letting, and will let your poets die of
hunger, continue to buy your poetry editions of the classics and to frame
photographs of the "Sistine Madonna" over your mantel-shelves. You know
quite well that vital art bores you and you have never understood it.[7]

Apart from the early Davidson essay, Flecker's literary criticism is
a conventional enough expression of the "art-for-art's sake" point of
view, reflecting the theory which lies behind most of his verse. Even
the early piece about Davidson forecasts Flecker's later development
because, in his insistence on that poet's "objectivity," he has written
the prelude to his more fully orchestrated praise of the allied doctrines of Parnassianism and "art for art's sake."

II   The Visionary Fantasies

More important than Flecker's literary criticism are his visionary
fantasies, most notably "The Last Generation" which was originally
published in The Best Man while he was still at Oxford. In this story
about a revolt led by a young poet-prophet, Joshua Harris, who is
distressed by the ugliness of the modern world, decides to assume
control of it. The revolt succeeds; a proclamation is issued; and the
important part of it relates to the sterilization of women as a
deliberate means of bringing the human race to an end. As the pop-
ulation declines, a group of young people of "taste," the "last
generation," forms a club, the Florentine League, and withdraws to
a garden, determined "to live apart from the rest of the world" like
"that merry company of gentlefolk of Boccaccio's Decameron who,
when the plague was raging at Florence, left the city, and retiring to
a villa in the hills, told each other enchanting tales."[8]
The young people, who read poetry and cultivate the arts, remain
in the garden until their thirty-seventh year; then most of the
members decide to commit suicide rather than join the ugly world

outside, as they are forced to do by a rule established by the league's founders. Eventually, only one remains; but, just as he is about to take poison and join his dead companions, the cup is wrenched from his hand by a "terrific blast," and "a wave of despair and loneliness" sweeps over him, causing him to exclaim: "What am I doing among these dead aesthetes? Take me back to the country where I was born, to the house where I am at home, to the things I used to handle, to the friends with whom I talked, before men went mad. I am sick of this generation that cannot strive or fight, these people of one idea, this doleful, ageing world. Take me away."[9] Whereupon the wind wafts him over the wall of the garden, back to the crude outside world. There he finds that the majority of those still alive have become depraved; there is scarcely a face that "was not repulsively deformed with the signs of lust, cunning and debauch,"[10] and soon the last survivor of the Florentine League finds himself at one with them. Gradually, the human race dies out, the buildings crumble, but life remains, "myriads of brown, hairy, repulsive little apes" emerging from the ruins," one of them building a fire with sticks."[11]

Although "The Last Generation" is something of a *jeu d'esprit*, very much the sort of thing a clever Oxford undergraduate in the early 1900s might be expected to write, it does have serious undertones: it serves as another reminder that, though Flecker may have subscribed to the doctrine of art for art's sake, he was far from being one of its more extravagantly melancholic, nihilistic exponents. Inspired by Max Nordau's *Degeneration* (1895),[12] a somewhat hysterical, pseudoscientific diatribe against the art-for-art's-sake movement, and perhaps influenced by reading Samuel Butler's *Erewhon* (1892), a book very much in vogue at Oxford while Flecker was there,[13] "The Last Generation" draws attention to the futile consequences of an existence devoted to art rather than to life. To withdraw from life may provide a pleasurable escape from the ugliness of one's surroundings, but such an act is ultimately self-defeating. Life goes on just the same. This Flecker knew; and, though he died young, his realization of the futility of withdrawal saved him perhaps from the fate of such people as Ernest Dowson and others of that group referred to by W. B. Yeats in his *Autobiography* as "the tragic generation."

In another of Flecker's visionary fantasies, "N'Jawk,"[14] the Esthetes appear rather better than they do in "The Last Generation." The story, such as it is, is about Peter Puxley, who "believed neither in Inspiration nor in Immortality, nor even in . . .

sweet Idealism," but his rationalist bent had not had a deleterious effect on his morals for "his character was steady and firm." He enters the church, but dies from a fit of cholic while still young. His soul, propelled through infinity, becomes entangled with the ghost of Slimbert, an Esthete poet and the author of "an exquisite volume of verse in the Doreskin Library of Modern Masterpieces" and of several unsigned essays on "How to make money by writing," published in *Tit-Bits* and *Pearson's Weekly.* The two souls succeed in extricating themselves from one another, but they are captured and transported to an Oriental palace where they are ushered into the presence of the god N'Jawk who, finding Puxley has never done anything to honor him, orders that he be made into porridge. Meanwhile, Slimbert, by dint of extravagant flattery and hypocrisy, avoids Puxley's fate; and he is allowed to spend the rest of eternity with the young ladies of N'Jawk's court.

Though shorter than "The Last Generation," "N'Jawk" is somewhat similar; it was also influenced by Samuel Butler, this time by his *Erewhon Revisited* (1901), whose Chapter XVI on the dangerous limitations of rationalism seems to have left its mark. Puxley's name is clearly derived from the names of two eminent Victorian thinkers, Thomas Henry Huxley and Edward Bouverie Pusey, the former associated with the Rationalists and the latter with the Anti-Rationalists. Obviously, there is a little of both Huxley and Pusey in Flecker's creation; but one should not assume that Flecker is mounting a serious attack against these two men and the beliefs they stand for. Rather, Flecker's intention seems to have been to ridicule both the rational and the antirational approach to religion, for it is quite possible that there is no God at all; or, if there is, he may be quite different from what one imagines him to be, in which case all those agonizing, self-engrossing nineteenth-century controversies about faith and morality are rather ridiculous. Survival will be granted to the clear-sighted opportunists.

Another prose piece belonging to this group is "Pentheus,"[15] also written from the freethinker's position. The story derives from Euripides' *Bacchae,*[16] specifically Gilbert Murray's rhymed translation of the play, in which were included several notes concerning the cult of Dionysus that refer to the resurrection of the god and the affinity of this event with the coming of Christ.[17] Flecker's fantasy describes how Pentheus, "a harsh and surly tyrant," is alarmed by the revelry encouraged by Dionysus, especially after learning that his own mother has fallen under the god's spell; and he decides to attack him. He fails; and, before being torn limb from limb, he is made to appear ridiculous by performing "a drunken parody of the divine exaltation" which characterizes Dionysus' true followers. Pentheus, however, finds immortality; and at a later date the ancient confrontation between Pentheus and Dionysus is re-enacted. This time Dionysus, not Pentheus, meets disaster; but the god rises again and Pentheus, having had the worst of the exchange, endeavors to make friends with him and stipulates "that the dancing should be more private, and that the Maenads and Satyrs should be less eccentrically clothed." He also insists that the mystic feasts to the god be relegated to the seventh day when the initiants should be taught their duty to Pentheus; during the remaining six days, they are to be kept "at the bitter loom." Pentheus succeeds in turning religion into support of his own power, and the joy that once characterized Dionysian worship entirely disappears.

Then, continues Flecker, some time later a new god of liberty and war comes on the scene; and he destroys Pentheus; but, like Dionysus, Pentheus also proves to be indestructible. Rather more affable than previously, he has lived on in a new guise, that of a respectable, moral idealist. Unfortunately, his well-meaning philanthropy is just as much a grim parody of divine goodness as his tipsy jollity was a mockery of divine exaltation; and, though "his humdrum days may be pleasant or painful, he has never tasted of our purple grapes of heavy sorrow, our golden grapes of superhuman joy. Alas, poor Pentheus!"

The meaning of this fantasy is clear. It is a paean to holy joy at the expense of Puritan conscience, an indictment of the pietistic, well-washed idealism of the Victorian bourgeoisie, and a plea for "life" over morality. It is also a declaration of faith in the kind of life Flecker himself wished to lead, as well as an attack on the moral and spiritual values associated with his father. Together with "The Last Generation" and "N'Jawk," "Pentheus" reflects the most appealing side of Flecker's personality, his vitality and his enthusiasm for the world in which he lived, an enthusiasm, moreover, which transcended even the claims of art.

III *Educational Theory and Practical Application*

Flecker's vitality and enthusiasm are also reflected in his dialogue on educational theory, "The Grecians," and in his textbook for the study of Italian, *The Scholars' Italian Book;* but in both works their presence mitigates the effectiveness these books might have had as serious educational documents. The latter was composed while Flecker was at Constantinople, and he at first jocularly proposed to call it *Italian for Gentlemen*.[18] Evidently written in a spirit of gay condescension, facetiousness is never far away; and the amused, faintly contemptuous tone of the preface, however refreshingly original, must have alienated a number of schoolmasters who might have considered using the book. Flecker says his object in the book is "to enable any intelligent student who knows some Latin and French to learn with the minimum of labour to read a great literature"; then, making an ironic thrust at previous compilers of Italian grammars, he suggests that they have been "tormented by the dire necessity of filling up a large book on a simple subject." Finally, he says, "I express the hope that some Headmasters may find this book a useful recreation for a sixth form exhausted by successful labours in scholarship hunting."[19]

The main part of the book is divided into two sections: the first, a brief review of Italian grammar; the second, an anthology of passages followed by translations into English. Geraldine Hodgson insists that Flecker was keenly interested in his Italian textbook,[20] but one wonders whether his interest extended beyond the translations themselves. Flecker enjoyed translating, much as he enjoyed writing poetry: both were agreeable exercises of the imagination and the intellect. It is possible, therefore, that, having rendered a number of pieces of Italian prose and verse into English, Flecker decided to make them the core of an Italian language manual and to add the brief review of grammar in an attempt to give his book both organic unity and functional purpose.

On the other hand, this view may be unjust because Flecker was interested enough in education to write a book on educational theory, one in which he establishes as his ideal the humane, aristocratic spirit which informs the gifted amateurism of *The Scholars' Italian Book*. The contempt for "scholarship-hunting" is present, and the educational program he recommends is the kind in which his Italian language manual might be used.

"The Grecians," cast in the form of a Platonic dialogue, contains, in fact, Plato's theory of education as developed in *The Republic* but brought up to date. There is, however, an essential difference between Plato's notion of the function of education and Flecker's. Plato wishes to educate men to discover and appreciate truth; Flecker wishes to educate men to appreciate beauty. Plato's dialogue is the work of a philosopher who also happens to be a poet; Flecker's is that of a poet who tries hard to be a philosopher. The epigraph for "The Grecians" could have been taken from Flecker's preface to *The Golden Journey to Samarkand:* "It is not the poet's business to save a man's soul, but to make it worth saving." If one substitutes educator for poet, one has the philosophical basis on which Flecker's dialogue is constructed. Throughout his treatise, the emphasis is on the cultivation of the mind and the body as a way to appreciating the glory and beauty of the world; only passing attention is paid to moral education or preparation for a professional career.

Following Walter Pater in the conclusion to *The Renaissance,* Flecker relegates philosophy to a relatively minor role, noting that "we may find a pure philosopher very deficient in his appreciation of the joy of life," and "the joy of life is the heritage of those who have unlocked the secret door that leads into the garden of the senses."[21] Some boys, Flecker concedes, are incapable of appreciating "the mysteries and beauties of life,"[22] and these will be given a special kind of technical training. As for those of "the most refined intelligence," Flecker proposes an unashamedly elitist form of education, designed to produce cultivated aristocrats: "In an ideal state these boys would not have to earn their living: they would automatically become rulers of the State, or else be subsidised to live in leisure as artists or critics. In our actual England we can give this complete education only to the sons of the rich, and to those few boys which our school funds enable us to support, not only here but afterwards. To give a boy this complete education, we must keep him until he is at least twenty-one."

Curiously, however, Flecker is not in favor of allowing such students to absorb the education they receive, free from the petty tyranny of examiners:

An examiner may be stupid and set worthless papers; but provided the papers be well set, examination is the sole adequate test of a boy's capacity. For we have no sympathy with Cecil Rhodes, nor with the cheerful, popular, and chiefly ignorant crowds who come to Oxford under his fantastic testament: we do not like this democratic selection of the prize favourites: we pin our faith to a written and evident intellectual superiority. We mistrust the boy who is said to be 'very good at work really, but no use at exams.' Such a boy is either morally deficient that he cannot rise to a crisis and concentrate his energy and ideas — and far be it from me to admit such a one to be a Grecian — or else it means that he is incapable of literary composition or self-expression; or else that his thoughts and facts are so confused that he cannot write them down. There is a great deal wrong with boys who fail at examinations.[23]

These are strong words from a man whose career was punctuated by a series of failed examinations!

Flecker's superior students would be required to devote their days "to the culture of the mind" — to be schooled most intensively in "literature, representation and music." Contrary to Edwardian practice, Flecker would not have his students devote the greater part of their time studying the Classics, and he would not overburden them with grammar. "Three hours a week for three years" he regards as sufficient for both Latin and Greek, and he suggests that Classical instruction not be given to students before they are sixteen, at an age, in short, when they may be expected to "obtain a fuller understanding of the classic spirit than those to whom Latin and Greek are a ceaseless drudgery and evil." If the Classics are taught in this way, Flecker believes, students will learn, "no less than others have learnt, from these time-honoured studies, that calm and even fervour of mind, that same and serene love of beautiful things, that freedom from religious bigotry and extravagance which marks the writings of the Greeks, and that seriousness, decorum, and strength, that sense of arrangement and justice which marks the writings and still more the history of the Romans."[24]

The main reason for learning a language, Flecker believes, is not to converse or write in it but to read its literature. After all, he says, "any German clerk . . . any cosmopolitan or Swiss innkeeper, any half-breed dragoman can gabble six or seven tongues, and sometimes gabble them correctly; and the dreariest lady student from Russia can speak beautiful French and passable German, and yet not have in her head a single Russian not to speak of German or French, idea."[25] Students should strive for a level of linguistic proficiency which will enable them to read literature swiftly and with pleasure.

Flecker's choice of literary works for study is somewhat unconventional. Not surprisingly, considering his Parnassian inclinations, Leconte de Lîsle's *Poèmes Barbares* is strongly recommended; Corneille and Racine are ignored — after all, one would not expect "to interest a Frenchman in English by presenting him with *Paradise Lost*";[26] but Honoré de Balzac and Anatole France are given special commendation. Among German literary works, *Faust*, Book I; Heine; Sudermann; and Nietzsche are all recommended; in Italian, he would have his boys read "a great deal of Dante, a little of Petrarch," some Boccaccio, Matteo Bandello, Masuccio of Salerno, Carlo Goldoni, and Gabriele d'Annunzio, as well as several lesser known writers.[27]

In emphasizing the representative arts, Flecker considers doing so his most revolutionary proposal. He wishes to train his students "to notice things in pictures"; "to regard nature from an artistic point of view"; and "to represent things for themselves."[28] The true end of art education, he says, is to make students realize that the great picture is not necessarily one which portrays a heroic or pathetic subject, for technique should be the sole criterion. He would have his students draw and paint, however clumsily, not merely for the purpose of making exact copies of objects or other paintings, but for the sheer joy of "inventing for himself or imitating nature."[29] He would also expose them not only to great art (not merely that which is generally acknowledged to be great) but also to the French Impressionists, to examples of Japanese prints, to Persian miniatures, and to Indian bronzes.[30]

Flecker admits that his enthusiasm for music is less than his enthusiasm for the representative arts, but he would have his students understand "the aim and structure of classical music." As for history, mathematics, and science, these should be relegated to subsidiary status. History he finds a "specious substitute for liberal education in the arts"; but he acknowledges that it could be "most useful as a pleasant and instructive afternoon diversion for those not very intelligent boys who are working to enter a trade or profession." Unlike Plato, Flecker thinks little of mathematics, suggesting that his "Grecians" be compelled "to learn sufficient mathematics to prevent their being put to shame in the affairs of life, and no more, unless they specially desire it." However, what he says about the teaching of mathematics would find sympathy among the advocates of "new math," because, since he deplores the laborious working out of mechanical exercises, he suggests that a good mathematics teacher should endeavor to interest his class in "the delight he himself takes in mathematical problems, by selecting the most fascinating and important examples of mathematical method." As for the natural sciences, these "if unaccompanied by other studies [are] poor training for the mind"; therefore, Flecker does not believe that his students should be "expected to do more than attend two weekly lectures delivered in non-technical language on scientific laws." There should be a museum at the school, but it should not be cluttered with exotic novelties; it should be a "neat and systematic collection of local flora and fauna."[31]

The school itself should be situated near the sea, preferably on the Hampshire Downs. The buildings should not be "Splendid Gothic," the traditional design of most educational establishments, but should be "after the American manner" — constructed with an eye for "comfort and utility," their beauty deriving "not from the added or-namentation of an antique style, but from the principles of symmetry and design." Physical exercise would be encouraged, not by forcing the children into team sports, but by allowing them to pursue the athletic activity in which they show the most proficiency. Corporal punishment would be allowed because, says Flecker, "I consider the sentimentalist more poisonous than the flagellant," and sexual intimacies among the boys should be discouraged by having each boy possess "a book on the subject" that contains "the exact truth without exaggerating dangers or threatening hell."[32]

"The Grecians" proposes an impractical system of education; and, though many modern educators would doubtless agree with Flecker's views about school-building design and about physical exercise, they would hardly agree with his emphasis on the humanities at the almost total exclusion of the pure and applied sciences. An interesting document, it is, perhaps, something of an apologia for Flecker's conspicuous lack of academic success; and, as Douglas Goldring has pointed out, its main interest lies in the fact that it throws considerable light on the man who wrote it.[33] In "The Grecians," Flecker describes a system of education calculated to produce a humane dilettante with decidedly nonconformist proclivities, rather than a useful, disciplined, industrious member of society — to produce, in fact, a man very like Flecker himself. In other words, what Flecker seems to have unconsciously sought to achieve in "The Grecians" is moral and theoretical justification for his own behavior and way of life.

As a child, Flecker was constantly at odds with the restrictive routines of the schools he attended; and he was always running into trouble as a result of his inability to conform to the corporate discipline of these institutions. He had little respect for members of the teaching profession; he compares them in "The Grecians" with businessmen to the latter's advantage.[34] In the same book he describes their appearance at a special service held in a certain public school. There they were, writes Flecker, "some two hundred head and assistant masters. A more tragic sight I have never seen." "Usually," Flecker continues, "schoolmasters are surrounded by boys and one does not notice what a sorry sight they are, but *en masse* they look positively ill." So it was, in this congregation, they made a depressing sight: "I saw men who had failed, whose lips were hard, and their faces drawn and sallow, [and] when I remarked the imbecile athletes who taught football and puny scientists who expounded the dark mystery of nature, the sapless scholars who taught Plato and Catullus by the page and hour, the little wiry-bodied men in spectacles who trained their pupils in *King Lear* for the Cambridge Locals, I shuddered and felt faint."[35]

This description was too much for Flecker's long-suffering parents, and his father refused to discuss "The Grecians" with his son, "seeing in it nothing but a jeer," an understandable if unjust estimate of the dialogue when one realizes that the congregation which Flecker had described was one which he and his father had attended at Cheltenham.[36] That Flecker should have included this passage is evidence of his tactlessness and bad taste; more important, however, it strongly suggests that his integrity as an educational theorist is questionable since one cannot help feeling that "The Grecians" was as much occasioned by Flecker's desire to attack his father and all the educational values he stood for, as it was by a desire to propound a serious, sincerely held educational philosophy. It is almost as if Flecker wrote his dialogue in an attempt to embarrass his father and, at the same time, to provide himself with an alibi to account for his failure. "Look," he appears to be saying "how could you have expected me to achieve anything worthwhile, considering the unenlightened education you gave me."

IV The King of Alsander

The King of Alsander, though not a successful novel, is Flecker's most ambitious prose work. A curious, picaresque tale which mixes high romance and social commentary, it is awkwardly constructed, uncertain in tone, and inconsistent in its characterization; the style wobbles uncertainly between purple prose and undergraduate facetiousness. The hero of the novel, Norman Price, is the son of a country-town grocer; and one day, while working in his father's shop, he meets an old man who enjoins him to run away from home and visit the wonderful land of Alsander. Norman steals some of his father's money for his journey, and he soon arrives at his destination where he meets a charming young girl called Peronella. The two fall in love, much to the chagrin of Peronella's present lover, Cesano; and Norman takes up lodging in her house under the watchful eye of her widowed mother. One day Norman visits the Royal Castle and learns of the recent history of Alsander. It seems that a previous monarch, King Basilandron, much addicted to revelry, one day staged an elaborate Bacchic orgy, and the neighboring state of

Ulmreich seized this occasion to invade Alsander. Alsander retained its independence, but its power declined; and, under the reign of Basilandron's successor, King Andrea, who was insane, the country degenerated even more, thanks largely to the corrupt Regency of Duke Vorza, who governed Alsander less for the welfare of its people than for personal gain and enjoyment of a ruler's prerogatives.

During this time Norman appears on the scene and is drawn into a conspiracy by the so-called Society for the Advancement of Alsander which aims to place Norman on the throne instead of the mad Andrea, whom nobody has seen because he is locked up in his own castle. Encouraged by a young man called Arnolfo, Norman works to overthrow Vorza; the plot succeeds; Norman becomes king and pretends to be Andrea, miraculously cured after treatment in England; and a chastened Vorza is bought off by being made Lord Chamberlain. After the coronation, Arnolfo reveals that he is not really a young man, but a girl who is really the exiled Princess Ianthe and who has determined to make Norman her husband. Meanwhile, Peronella discovers a letter which clearly reveals that Norman is an imposter; when she brings it to the attention of Vorza, a counterplot is begun to depose Norman and restore Andrea. There is a battle during which both Vorza and Andrea are conveniently killed, and Norman triumphs, marries Princess Ianthe, and begins to rule Alsander with justice and intelligence. Peronella disappears from Alsander, never to be seen again.

The King of Alsander was probably begun while Flecker was still at Oxford, and it was completed only a few months before his death. In 1906, Douglas Goldring heard Flecker read parts of it; and, under the spell of Flecker's personality, he thought the novel to be remarkably good,[37] an opinion he later modified considerably. In the summer of 1906, Flecker lost the first three chapters of the manuscript while on his way to Paris;[38] and, though he managed to rewrite most of what he had lost, he admitted in November, 1907, in a letter to Frank Savery that "the novel goeth slowly."[39] Early in 1908, he completed a first draft;[40] and, for a while, it seemed as though John Dent would publish it.[41] The publisher evidently rejected the manuscript for in January, 1912, Martin Secker had agreed to publish it, subject to extensive revision.[42] The revision Flecker found a "dreadful trial,"[43] and he was soon convinced that only the first two chapters had some merit.[44] "Nothing in God's earth," he wrote to Frank Savery, "can infuse any reality into the tale; so I confine myself to polishing and writing it up less heavily and hope it may be a popular success."[45]

Flecker's first revision was not acceptable to Secker, and he asked him to revise the manuscript again, which Flecker did; but, by the time the revision had been completed, Secker had lost interest in the novel. In June, 1913, Flecker wrote to Douglas Goldring to ask if he should take Secker to court and to solicit his aid in finding another publisher. By this time, Flecker had convinced himself that *The King of Alsander* was really "a very jolly and fantastic work,"[46] and Max Goschen also seems to have felt it had merit because he eventually agreed to publish it. The novel appeared early in 1914, some months before Flecker's death.

Considering the long and unfortunate history of the novel's composition, its several false starts and revisions, it is not surprising that *The King of Alsander* is, in Goldring's phrase, "a patchy affair."[47] But, even if the novel's passage into print had been smoother, it is doubtful whether Flecker would have been able to create an organic work of art since he seems to have derived his plot from a number of existing literary sources rather than from his own imagination, and the separate influences are clearly traceable. The idea of a conspiracy to substitute a young Englishman for a native monarch is reminiscent of Antony Hope's popular novel *The Prisoner of Zenda* (1894); but, unlike Hope, Flecker never expects the reader to take his outrageous plot seriously. The most obvious influence, however, is Apuleius' *Golden Ass*, "that mysterious wonder-story" written in a "glittering precious style"[48] which Norman takes with him on his travels. From this work Flecker appears to have derived the notion of an episodic narrative which enables the main character to satirize some of the vices and follies of humankind. Moreover, the endings of the two works are remarkably similar: the miraculous appearance of the "white woman" in *The King of Alsander* recalls the intervention of the goddess Isis who restores Apuleius to human form. *Zuleika Dobson* (1911), Max Beerbohm's amusingly told tale of the devastating effects of a young adventuress on the students at Oxford, also seems to have been an influence, as well as Voltaire's *Candide*. Few of the characters involved in Flecker's plot linger in the memory with the possible exception of the eccentric consul, who was probably drawn from life in spite of the author's disclaimer that all the characters in *The King of Alsander* are "purely fictitious."[49] The others are cardboard caricatures, reminding one of the characters of a Ruritanian musical comedy.

For many readers the most interesting feature of the novel is the insight it provides into Flecker's likes and dislikes, his attitudes and views about literature and life in general. For example, one learns that the author thinks highly of Joseph Conrad's *Youth*;[50] that Damascus is "a very filthy town with electric trams and no drains";[51] that in "no tale since *Tom Jones* have we had an honest Englishman who makes love because it is jolly and he doesn't care."[52]

"There is also a highly revealing disgression on the excellence of whipping." Here Flecker once more returns to a subject which exerted a powerful, if unhealthy, fascination for him. In "Taoping," he describes a flagellation scene;[53] in *Hassan*, Pervaneh and Rafi are whipped;[54] in his essay "The Grecians," he advocates judicious flogging in the upbringing of young boys.[55]

However, nowhere else in Flecker's writing is flagellation treated so extensively as it is in *The King of Alsander*. Flecker considers the role of the whip in Spartan and Roman times, in the East, and then moves on to consider the literary aspect of whipping, concluding that there is "no great book without its whipping."[56] He admits that he would rather see adults whipped than children, and the episode concludes with a description of Norman's experience when the executioner lays on "steadily and evenly" until the back of the future king of Alsander "looked like a sheet of music paper."[57]

That Flecker's interest in flagellation was more than theoretical is apparent from his having had a lengthy, intense discussion on the subject with T. E. Lawrence, when he came to visit the Fleckers in Areiya.[58] More pointedly, from Flecker's correspondence with his wife it is clear that caning and being tied up and caned formed an essential part of his married love-making. Thus, in one of Flecker's letters to Hellé from Smyrna shortly after his engagement, he presses her to lose no time in coming to stay with him, adding that he will "keep the little black strap" and make "the loveliest red marks" on her when she comes. Whenever she may be displeased with him, he adds, she "could tie him up and have a glorious revenge."[59] As for *The King of Alsander* there is little in it to recommend itself to most readers. The narrative runs along briskly enough; there is the occasional amusing comment or turn of phrase, as for example the old man's remark that he is quite unimpressed by Norman's "Watts-Dunton talk" after hearing that his dreams are his best friends.[60] But it is difficult to justify a novel's worth in these terms; and, while it might have seemed moderately impressive coming from an undergraduate, it is not especially noteworthy from a supposedly mature man of letters.

Flecker's prose as a whole does little to enhance his reputation. His literary criticism is intelligent but not especially distinguished;

his visionary fantasies and treatises on education are interesting
mainly for the light they throw on his ideas and personality; and *The
King of Alsander* would have been forgotten entirely if it had not
been written by a man who had attracted attention as a poet and as a
dramatist. Flecker was a writer who enjoyed manipulating words
and meters for their own sake, and his genius found its most effective
expression in verse; his prose has its merits, but only an ardent
Flecker enthusiast would claim that it deserved more than passing
attention.

CHAPTER 5

The Drama

I *Verse Drama as a Literary Form*

ALTHOUGH Flecker is a better poet than a dramatist, he is
perhaps better known not for his poetry but for his play *Hassan,* one of the few successful verse dramas of the twentieth century
before T. S. Eliot's *Murder in the Cathedral* (1935). Though
Flecker's other verse play, *Don Juan,* is not so successful as *Hassan,*
it is nonetheless an interesting excursion into a genre modern examples of which have rarely attained higher status than that of
literary curiosities. Why good modern verse drama should be so difficult to write is not clear. After all, a strong native tradition of verse
drama exists, and in recent years many critics and theorists of the
form have suggested what the verse dramatist should strive for in his
productions. T. S. Eliot in his essay "On Poetry and Drama" (1950),
for example, has described the general aim of poetic drama and has
provided some guiding principles, based on his own experience, for
would-be verse dramatists. "Poetic drama," he wrote, "comes
closest to expressing those things which usually music alone can express." But, he continues,

We can never emulate music, because to arrive at the condition of music
would be the annihilation of poetry, and especially of dramatic poetry.
Nevertheless, I have before my eyes a kind of mirage of the perfection of
verse drama, which would be a design of human action and of words, such as
to present at once the two aspects of dramatic and musical order. . . . To go
as far in this direction as it is possible to go, without losing that contact with
the ordinary, everyday world with which drama must come to terms, seems
to me the proper aim of dramatic poetry, for it is ultimately the function of
art, in imposing a credible order upon an ordinary reality, and thereby
eliciting some perception of an order *in* reality, to bring us to a condition of
serenity, stillness and reconciliation, and then leave us, as Virgil left Dante,
to proceed toward a region where that guide can avail us no farther.[1]

George Wilson Knight's description of the effect the poetic dramatist should strive for is quite similar: "We should not look for perfect verisimilitude to life, but rather see each play as an expanded metaphor, by means of which the original vision has been projected into forms roughly corresponding with actuality, conforming thereto with greater or less exactitude according to the demands of its nature. . . . The persons, ultimately, are not human at all, but purely symbols of poetic vision."[2]

Finally, W. B. Yeats, recounting his intentions as a verse dramatist and having in mind the program of the Abbey Theatre to promote specifically Irish drama, said: "I want to get back to primary ideas. I want to put the old stories into verse, and if I put them into dramatic verse, it will matter less to me henceforward who plays them than what they play, and how they play it. I want to get our heroic age into verse."[3]

All three writers affirm the desirability of the verse dramatist's being able to project a special kind of world which hovers between physical and spiritual reality, between speech and music. Eliot calls it a "mirage" between "poetry" and "music"; George Wilson Knight calls it "metaphor"; Yeats means, though he does not so name it, "myth." Clearly, considerable unanimity of opinion exists among these three writers as to what kind of reality the verse dramatist should endeavor to present. However, if one looks at a representative selection of Victorian and twentieth-century verse dramas, many of which clearly aspire to metaphor rather than to direct representation, one is bound to admit that few may be considered successful.

Some verse dramas fail because they are little more than costume pieces; they are plays in naturalistic settings, written in verse in an attempt to make them seem archaic; they are simply self-conscious attempts to turn the clock back and to recreate the world of the romantic past. To this category belongs Oscar Wilde's *The Duchess of Padua* (1891), a drama written in a pseudo-Shakespearian style, such as that burlesqued by Max Beerbohm in "Savonarola Brown."[4] Plays of this kind fail because they are little more than Victorian melodramas with historical plots which are written in blank verse. There is no attempt to penetrate surface reality; and no attempt is made to universalize the characters and action, — to give them mythic significance. They are simply realistic dramas set in the past.

At the other extreme, some verse dramas fail because they are really dramatic poems. To this group belong Matthew Arnold's

Merope (1858), Tennyson's *Becket* (1884), Robert Bridges' eight classical dramas,[5] and Harley Granville-Barker's adaptation of Thomas Hardy's *Dynasts*. Unlike the pseudo-Shakespearian dramas, which use poetry, paradoxically, to add verisimilitude — it being improperly assumed that everyone in high society living before 1700 spoke in blank verse — the second category of verse drama uses actors and scenery to give life to the poetry. The former fails to escape from the restrictive conventions of realistic drama, the latter from the conventions of the printed page. Neither kind succeeds in projecting the stage reality for which T. S. Eliot called — that shadow world which lies somewhere between prose and music.

Some dramatists at the turn of the century, however, did attempt to do something more than write realistic dramas in verse, or verse for the stage; and one of the most popular was Stephen Phillips (1864 - 1915). Phillips had a tremendous success as a verse dramatist in his day; his *Paolo and Francesca* (1899), *Herod* (1900), *Nero* (1902), and *Ulysses* (1902) in particular attracted widespread attention. Phillips was an actor before he became a dramatist, and his plays reveal an awareness of the exigencies of theatrical presentation. Though he endeavored to bring back English tragedy to the severe classicism of the Greeks, thereby purging it of Elizabethan "luxuriance," he could not prune his somewhat florid diction. His plays, as a result, are actable without being especially dramatic; his lines scan, but one could hardly call them great poetry. Avoiding the excesses of such plays as *The Duchess of Padua* on the one hand and Granville-Barker's adaptation of Hardy's *Dynasts* on the other, Phillips' plays are a compromise between two extremes rather than extended metaphors in dramatic form.

Phillips' verse dramas are all set in the past, and the historical distance of their subject matter sanctions the use of poetry. The problem is: can contemporary subject matter be successfully portrayed in verse drama? After writing *Murder in the Cathedral*, Eliot realized that he had not settled the problem of whether verse drama was a genuinely viable twentieth-century literary form. The historical subject — and especially the cathedral setting, which made ritual and formal, rhythmic utterance appropriate, all made his task as a verse dramatist easier than it might otherwise have been; therefore, he decided to write a poetic drama which would be truly contemporary in terms of its subject matter, setting, and diction. Consequently, Eliot's next play, *The Family Reunion* (1937), was certainly more "modern" than *Murder in the Cathedral*, but it was probably less successful. Moreover, his verse dramas which followed certainly gained in contemporaneity but only at the expense of poetry; and his last play, *The Elder Statesman* (1958), is hardly poetic in any real sense of the word. Judging by Eliot's experience, verse drama is not a viable twentieth-century literary form unless special circumstances, such as in *Murder in the Cathedral*, enable the dramatist to use verse without any sense of its being inappropriate to the setting or subject.[6]

Eliot's experience is corroborated by Flecker's: his "contemporary" play *Don Juan* is a failure; and his *Hassan*, like *Murder in the Cathedral*, succeeds because of special circumstances that relate to its setting and its production. The most effective parts of *Don Juan*, moreover, are those immediately after the shipwreck when Don Juan and Tisbea fall in love.[7] This romantic episode has a faintly archaic quality which makes its presentation in verse seem appropriate. In other parts of the play — those in which Flecker introduces such contemporary issues as workers' rights and the ethics of war — verse seems inappropriate.

II *Don Juan*

Flecker's interest in the story of Don Juan seems to have begun around 1910, for his translation of Baudelaire's "Don Juan aux enfers"[8] was among the six new pieces included in *Forty-Two Poems* (1911). Also, Hellé Flecker recalls that in November, 1910, she received from her husband a copy of a poem entitled "Don Juan from the Shadows," which contained in condensed form the subject of the later play. After "some polishing and compressing," it became "Don Juan Declaims";[9] and later still it was used as the closing piece of Act II of the completed play.[10] Around Christmas, 1910, Flecker decided to write a full-length play about Don Juan, the details of which he outlined in a letter to Frank Savery, to whom he also sent a copy of "Don Juan from the Shadows." At this time, he acknowledged that when he wrote his Don Juan poem he knew nothing of the legend; but soon afterwards he read Molière's "*marvellous* play," *Don Juan ou le festin de Pierre*, and "a French monograph of enormous length," *La légende de Don Juan* by Gendome de Brévotte.

Flecker's concept of a play about Don Juan began to form slowly, and he was able to announce details of his projected drama to Frank Savery: "Of course my conception will be modern. I shall portray D. J. utterly disappointed in his *grande passion*, seeking refuge from

sickly and decadent despair first in the world and in the passion for
humanity and justice, then questioning religion, then ordinary
morality until finally he becomes an utter sadist. Then comes the
statue, which is the miracle, to make him doubt reason itself, and he
dies bravely."[11]

With this plan in mind, Flecker worked hard on the play, writing
much of it in Paris while staying with his future wife before assum-
ing his post at Beirut. At this time he read G. A. Monypenny's *Life of
Disraeli* (1910),[12] and it seems likely that Monypenny's account of
Disraeli's decision to send the British fleet to the Dardanelles in
1877 in the face of cabinet opposition influenced the Embankment
scene in *Don Juan*[13] since Framlingham's decision to despatch gun-
boats first provokes Don Juan to remonstrate with the statesman and
later to kill him.

By March, 1911, the play was finished; and, though its theme
remained much as he had described it to Frank Savery, the
characterization of Don Juan had undergone a slight change; he now
had greater affinities with Byron's portrait of the character than
Molière's. Don Juan in the final version emerges as something of an
idealist who challenges society's conventions, but the influence of
Molière's more cynical portrayal is still there. The result is a
somewhat inconsistent character — almost as if the author could not
make up his mind whether his Don Juan was an idealistic reformer or
an aristocratic cad.

The play begins with a shipwreck, reminiscent of the opening
scene of Shakespeare's *The Tempest;* and Don Juan and a sailor
named Owen Jones are cast up on a rocky coast where they meet the
beautiful girl Tisbea. Tisbea and Don Juan fall in love in a scene
which recalls the Haidée episode in Canto II of Byron's *Don Juan.*
The focus then shifts to Gloucester where Flecker introduces Don
Juan's father, Don Pedro, and later a group of angry strikers led by
Robert Evans, whom Don Juan manages to pacify. At this point,
Don Juan rejects Tisbea because a man in his position should not be
running around with a peasant girl; later, one learns that she has
married Owen Jones who has become Don Juan's servant. Don Juan,
having once more taken his rightful place in society, is courting
Lady Isabella, the beautiful daughter of Lord Framlingham, the
Conservative prime minister; but he unknowingly has also won the
affection of Lady Anna, Lady Isabella's ugly sister.

Lord Framlingham reveals to Don Juan that England will soon be
at war; and Don Juan declares in the ensuing exchange his Socialist

sympathies, affirming that the whole of the British Empire is not worth the lives of the poor who will be sacrificed in battle for their country. When Lord Framlingham still insists that the country must go to war, Don Juan shoots him. In Act III, Lady Anna reveals her passion for Don Juan and also that she knows he is a murderer. Don Juan then shoots her in the presence of Lady Isabella, who declares she still loves him. At this moment the statue of the late Lord Framlingham enters to announce that, as Don Juan has "let loose murder on the world, which is war without honour," and has loved reason, caring for no one but himself, he too must die. Don Juan agrees with Lord Framlingham's judgment upon him, and the curtain falls with the hero's passing into "a rain of fire."

Like *The King of Alsander, Don Juan* is part romance and part Socialist tract. The characters are inconsistent too, especially Owen Jones and Lady Anna; the former behaves like a romantic idealist for part of the time and like a con man for the other; the latter is a virginal bluestocking during the first scenes in which she appears, and later an uninhibited sensualist. Act I is impossibly confused, for in it one meets Don Pedro who, in spite of his name, turns out to be a true English gentleman. He persuades Owen Jones to restore his son to him; he offers money to expedite the arrangement, which Jones refuses; then Jones bargains for and eventually receives more than the sum originally proposed. (Incidentally, it is not made clear why Don Pedro needs to bribe Owen Jones in the first place since Don Juan later returns to his father of his own free will.) At the beginning of the scene, Don Juan and Tisbea are wildly in love with each other; but, at the end of it he has rejected her, an event as unexpected as it is unprepared for. In the exchanges between Robert Evans and Don Juan, the hero plays the role of a gay, insouciant aristocrat who dresses down the lower classes for presuming to lay hands on a strikebreaker, a behavior curiously inconsistent with his later, impassioned plea on behalf of social justice in the scene on the Embankment with Lord Framlingham. Finally, there is the ludicrously sentimental and entirely inappropriate episode with the little girl to whom Don Juan tells a story, thus incurring her mother's displeasure since she has told her daughter never to speak to strangers. She then gives the girl a spanking, which Don Juan finds immensely amusing.

In an attempt to have his play produced, Flecker sent a copy of it on March 6, 1911, to George Bernard Shaw, who criticized parts of it but encouraged Flecker to continue writing for the stage. "I really don't know how to advise you about this play," wrote Shaw, "because it falls between not being good enough for the commercial theatre, and not bad enough to be scrapped." However, he continued,

There is no doubt in my mind that you have high qualifications for dramatic work — some of the highest in fact. I withdraw what I said about Pantomine verse: on reading the whole play I see nothing to complain of but a few careless verses. The worst scene is the argument of Don Juan with the labour leader, which is not knowledgeable. Evans is only a vague hotchpotch of the newspaper notions of half-a-dozen different types of crank and is not really conceived by you as a human being from his own point of view as the others are, though even he has a good passage or two. The last act contains one of the best scenes I have ever read — that with Tisbea. It is a stroke of genius.

You had better go on making a fool of yourself for ten years or so and see what will come of it. The battle is not certain to end in victory yet; for at your age people sometimes make astonishingly fine flashes in the pan that they never repeat. But with common sense and accurate knowledge of the world — tact and experience, to put it vulgarly — you ought to go far; for you certainly have the trump cards. Only do, for Heaven's sake, remember that there are plenty of geniuses about, and that the real difficulty is to find writers who are sober, honest, and industrious and have been for many years in their last situation.[14]

That Flecker should have chosen Shaw as his literary arbiter is not especially surprising; for, quite apart from Shaw's increasing eminence as a critic and as a dramatist, parts of Flecker's *Don Juan* reveal a close familiarity with Shaw's work, notably *Man and Superman* (1903). Flecker had, of course, been familiar with Shaw's work while he was at Cambridge; and he may even have met him during the time of his association with the Fabians; in May, 1909, he wrote to his parents about an evening spent discussing Shaw with "a set of the stupidest fools" he had ever met during the course of his university career.[15] More specifically, Flecker's Don Juan, a man who in the early stages of the play proclaims his allegiance to humanistic social principles, has clear affinities with Shaw's Don Juan in Act III of *Man and Superman*, who appears as the apostle of progress in whom all the social aspirations of the new century are enshrined. It is also worth observing that, in this scene in Shaw's play, a lengthy dialogue involves The Devil, Don Juan, The Statue, and his daughter Ana; and Shaw's Ana, rather shrewish, unromantic, and opinionated, is a fairly close relation of Flecker's Lady Anna before her infatuation with Don Juan. Finally, Lord Framlingham has something in him of Shaw's Andrew Undershaft in *Major Barbara* (1905); both characters believe in violence and war as the inevitable consequences of past history.[16]

Shaw, perhaps recognizing in *Don Juan* the influence of his own work, was kinder about the play's quality than he should have been. Certainly Flecker had a great deal of difficulty in finding someone to produce it. Herbert Trench, then manager of the Haymarket Theatre, London, expressed some interest in it, but this came to nothing. After receiving some advice from Frank Savery as to how the play could be improved — he suggested the omission of the scene in which Owen Jones extorts money from Don Pedro — Flecker began revising it.[17] In June, 1911, he wrote to John Mavrogordato, saying that he had revised the play;[18] and the following August in a letter to him, Flecker admits having sent his manuscript to Frank Harrison, Granville-Barker, and Mrs. Frederika Horniman of the Little Theatre, who produced mostly experimental plays or the work of unknown authors.[19]

Shaw had pointed to the possibility of the Little Theatre's producing *Don Juan*, a suggestion which then had no appeal for Flecker since he had hoped to see it on the commercial stage;[20] but, when even the Little Theatre was not interested in his play, Flecker shelved it; in the meantime, he had begun *Hassan*. By the time of Flecker's death, *Don Juan* had not found a producer; and, though the play was published in 1925, it was not staged until a year later at a 300 club performance on April 26 at the Court Theatre. The only other professional or semiprofessional production since that time has been the appropriately named Elroy Players of the Royal Academy of Dramatic Art, who staged it at St. George's Hall, London, from January 6 to January 17, 1947.

Don Juan cannot be regarded as other than a literary curiosity, though it does have some slight autobiographical interest. It may be that the inconsistency of Don Juan's behavior reflects the confusion in Flecker's own mind at the time of the play's composition. In 1911 Flecker was in a state of emotional uncertainty as a result of his broken engagement with Eleanor Finlayson, his infatuation with Leila Berkeley, and his growing involvement with Hellé. Flecker's behavior during this period was almost as confused as that of his hero. Unfortunately, he was unable to turn his personal experience to dramatic account, and Don Juan's erratic behavior is perhaps the play's greatest flaw. Even if Flecker had managed to overcome the obstacle of making his central character believable, it is doubtful whether the play would have received more critical attention than it has. It is not that the verse is mediocre — some of it, in fact, is as polished as any that Flecker wrote — and it is not simply that most of the characters are unconvincing. The main reason for its lack of success lies in the verse-drama form itself, which does not lend itself to contemporary subject matter. In this respect, it is surprising that Flecker did not heed the words of the writer he so much admired, John Davidson; for Davidson had stated categorically that the modern spirit was totally unsympathetic to verse drama as a form. "This age," Davidson wrote, "is too commercial, too entirely in the grip of economics: it is too immoderate in its pleasure in every kind of moral suggestion, every kind of temporary interest and ephemeral issue, to care for poetical drama." Furthermore, wrote Davidson, this age is "too abject in its haunt of dulcet romanticism, mystic piety and dwarfing comicality; and although the most tragic circumstances in the history of the world at our doors — the failure of Christendom, mainly — the mind, the imagination of our time is not yet healthy enough, not yet strong enough, not serious enough . . . not passionate enough, not great enough for tragedy."[21] However just or unjust Davidson's indictment of the modern age may be, *Don Juan* must be numbered among the many interesting but unsuccessful attempts by twentieth-century writers to compose verse drama based on contemporary themes and subject matter.

III   Hassan

Though Flecker seems to have ignored Davidson's warning about writing verse drama in the twentieth century, the latter's remarks about his own romantic farce, *Scaramouche at Naxos* (1888), could almost serve as a blueprint for what Flecker originally set out to achieve in *Hassan*. "True *Pantomime* is good-natured nightmare," Davidson wrote. In it "our sense of humour is titillated, and strummed, and kicked and oiled, and fustigated and stroked, and exalted and bedevilled, and, on the whole, severely handled by this self-same harmless incubus; and our intellectuals are scoffed at."[22] Davidson's words are not especially apt in relation to the final version of *Hassan*, but it seems more than probable that Flecker had initially intended to write a Middle Eastern pantomime, as may be seen from his own and his wife's comments about the genesis of his Oriental play.

Flecker first began to consider writing an Eastern play during his three-month stay on the island of Corfu from June to August, 1911.

Supposedly cured of the illness that had necessitated his confinement in Cranham sanitorium, Flecker was in good spirits; and he worked with enthusiasm on his Turkish in preparation for his forthcoming consular service examination. He also did a great deal of writing — his poems "Yasmin," "Saadabad," "The Hammam Name," "The Golden Journey," and "In Phaecia" were written at about this time — and read a number of books in Turkish, among them a volume of farcical plays. One of the plays he translated related the adventures of Hassan, a simple man, whose friends constantly played tricks on him with the aid of a Hebrew magician — a subject that so appealed to Flecker that he immediately sketched a short farce in which Zacchariah, the Jew, and love philters were the chief center of interest.[23]

The manuscript of this short farce no longer exists, but one can guess its substance; it was, no doubt, similar to the opening scenes in the final version of *Hassan*. About this time, Flecker had also been reading Dr. Joseph Charles Victor Mardrus' sixteen-volume French translation of *The Arabian Nights* (1898-1904), a rollicking, colorful rendering of the Oriental classic, the spirit of which Flecker endeavored to capture in his early farce. In this early version of the play, there was a woman called Yasmin; and, soon after he had finished it, he wrote a poem called "Yasmin: a Ghazel," which was incorporated into the final version of *Hassan*.[24]

Yasmin's name had suggested the song, and the song suggested a play, which prompted Flecker to consider writing a three-act comedy with Yasmin as the chief female character. About the same time, he wrote "A Diwan of the West," later published under the title "Prologue," in which the "Golden Journey to Samarkand" first appears. In June, 1911, Flecker wrote to John Mavrogordato, saying that he was working on his *Arabian Nights* play; and the following month he sent his three-act comedy to London to be typed. From this version, after much editing and revision, Flecker developed a five-act drama, the final version of *Hassan*.[25]

For the time being, Flecker did little to his play, only when his health broke and he was forced to enter the sanitarium at Leysin did he turn his attention to it once more. He began intense work on it; and in January, 1913, he sent a revised manuscript to Edward Marsh saying, "the hope of my life is in your hands."[26] Marsh was busy with the Georgian anthologies and did no more than glance at it; but, by the end of the month, he wrote to Flecker noting various ways in which he felt the play could be improved. The opening scene, he said, was poor and could be made better by eliminating some of the buffoonery. He also suggested that more use could be made of the beggars, and he complained that Hassan's character could be more "sharply defined."[27] Flecker agreed with some of Marsh's suggestions, and he wrote to Marsh in June, 1913, saying that he was "going to cut the farce clean out — or modify it greatly, and be less heavy with the Oriental expressions,"[28] a task which he had completed by August of the same year. Marsh then approached Granville-Barker with the manuscript, but he was too busy to read it, so he suggested that Flecker try John Drinkwater at the Birmingham Repertory Theatre instead.[29] Drinkwater looked at the manuscript, and, while Flecker awaited his verdict, he wrote to Marsh again, saying that he was not going "to worry over much about the requisites of the stage. A lot of rot is talked about literary plays not succeeding," he wrote; "I am only going to try and keep Hassan interesting; then if it's good enough the stage can adopt it or adapt itself to it."[30]

Eventually, Drinkwater rejected it; but Marsh managed to interest Basil Dean in Hassan. Dean saw that the play had potentialities, but he believed that it needed considerable compression, rearrangement, and rewriting; and he offered to undertake the revision himself. Flecker agreed but then decided he could do it better himself, saying that he was concerned about Dean's insistence on stage effect: "he imagines there is a difference between dramatic and literary criticism."[31] On June 18, 1914, Flecker wrote to Dean from Davos, where he was now staying, and enclosed a revised version of the play which he believed was "so immensely improved that it will require very little alteration." He also assured his correspondent that he would be amenable to suggestions for the play's improvement: "Please never think that I want to institute a sort of Literature V. Drama quarrel! For me every correction that makes the play more actable makes it better literature."[32] Flecker died on January 3, 1915, before Hassan could be revised completely, and the version which Dean eventually received had numerous corrections in the first half of the play, but none in the second. However, this manuscript was the basis for the text that was used when Hassan was staged at His Majesty's Theatre in September, 1923, and the version of Hassan that was published in 1922 was essentially the manuscript which Flecker had completed in August, 1913.

The changes which Flecker made in his several revisions of Hassan included the deletion of a number of characters: Yakub,

Hassan's friend; a Negro boy, Tulip; a woman, Splendour; and her three maids, Sugar Cane, Palm Branch, and Myrtle Blossom. In addition, Zaccharia, who originally appeared in person, is omitted, and only referred to, but never seen. On the other hand, two important characters in the published version, Pervaneh and Rafi, are not even mentioned in earlier versions; much of the dialogue, however, remained the same.[33] After he had expanded his play and sent it to England, Flecker wrote to Frank Savery on September 5, 1913, and described some of the changes and improvements he had made. He says that he means the newly introduced Pervaneh to be "a rather cold, fine woman . . . a sort of brave cowardly noble beast," and that the part of the play that thrills him most is the episode with the ghosts. He also notes that "Hassan originally was going to try and whip Yasmin not to kill her. But I decided that would be too sadistic, and not serious enough, so I altered it." He added, "I'm fond of the little scene of Yasmin and the Executioner."[34]

Later, although Flecker worried about some of the cuts which Dean suggested,[35] he seems to have approved them. In June, 1914, he wrote to Frank Savery about the latest revisions: "It's splendid; it really is. All the slow moving bits cut out, the language brightened, the end of Act IV immensely improved, and precious little lost by the cuts."[36] In the last revision Flecker made just before his death, Dean notes that the author had made a number of improvements in the scene in the House of the Moving Walls and in the encounter between Yasmin and Hassan in the pavilion. Dean also suggests that, had Flecker had more time to spend on the play, the Hassan-Yasmin and the Rafi-Pervaneh plots would have been more effectively integrated.[37]

Both the "published" and the "acting" versions of *Hassan* reveal how far Flecker had moved from his original source, for the farcical elements are overshadowed by the tragic, and the pantomime has been transformed into verse drama. In the strictly technical sense, of course, one has no right to call *Hassan* a verse drama because it is for the most part written in prose. Yet the total effect is as if it were a verse drama because the major part of the text could have been printed as free verse, in much the same way as W. B. Yeats reprinted Walter Pater's prose portrait of the Mona Lisa in *The Renaissance* as the first poem in his edition of *The Oxford Book of Modern Verse: 1892 - 1935.*[38] Indeed, the rich, incantatory prose of *Hassan* lends itself more readily to metrical analysis than Pater's passage, as may be seen from the following random example:

> Ishak, my heart is heavy, / and still the night
> drags on, / and still we wander in the
> crooked streets, / and still we find no
> entertainment, / and still the white moon
> shines.[39]

Therefore, although technically *Hassan* is not a verse drama, it falls most readily into that category; and it evokes the stage reality that lies between speech and music described by Eliot.

The plot concerns a middle-aged confectioner of Bagdad, Hassan, who has the misfortune to become infatuated with Yasmin, a beautiful but unscrupulous widow. Hassan goes to her home and recites some amorous verses before her window, and he becomes involved with Rafi and his band of ruffians, who are planning a conspiracy against the Caliph. Caliph Haroun-al-Raschid, as well as Jafar and Masrur, his Vizier and Executioner, respectively, and Hassan, are captured by Rafi who imprisons them in his headquarters, where he tells them of his plot to kill the Caliph in revenge for taking his mistress Pervaneh into his harem. Hassan effects their escape, and Rafi is taken prisoner; the Caliph acknowledges Hassan's assistance by making him second in the kingdom only to the Vizier and by giving him a pavilion in the palace garden; and Yasmin, who was uninterested in Hassan when he was a confectioner, now finds him a suitable lover. Hassan accepts her affection but does so with bitter self-contempt. When the Caliph passes judgment on Rafi and Pervaneh, he banishes the former and takes the latter as his wife; but, at the same time, he offers them an alternative fate: he will allow them twenty-four hours of love, at the end of which time they will be tortured and put to death. The lovers choose death; and Hassan, for presuming to plead on behalf of Pervaneh, is made to watch. The play ends with an embittered Hassan setting out on a pilgrimage with Ishak, the Court poet, to make the "Golden Journey to Samarkand."

A play such as *Hassan* obviously lends itself to spectacular production, and this is what it received from Basil Dean who staged it at His Majesty's Theatre, London, on September 23, 1923. The public's taste for Eastern spectaculars had previously been whetted by Oscar Asche's enormously popular *Chu Chin Chow*, which preceded *Hassan* at the same theater, opening on August 31, 1916, and closing on July 22, 1921. Obviously, if *Hassan* were to succeed, it would have to match the earlier production, and fortunately no expense was spared to make it a worthy successor to Asche's Oriental extravaganza.[40] The composer Frederick Delius was commissioned to write the music; Henry Ainley was engaged to play Hassan; Leon Quartermaine played Ishak; Cathleen Nesbitt played Yasmin; an enormous throng of extras swelled the already populous cast of characters, appearing as ambassadors, wrestlers, ghosts, mutes, dancing women, beggars, soldiers, police, attendants, merchants, camel-drivers, pilgrims, torturers, "casual loiterers," Jews, jesters, and calligraphists; Michel Fokine was commissioned to arrange dances for a corps de ballet; and George W. Harris was allowed a generous budget to design and execute the scenery and costumes.

As the opening night drew near, wrote Basil Dean, "public anticipation rose like a fever"; and "old playgoers remarked that nothing comparable had occurred since the great days of Irving and Tree." On the day of the dress rehearsal, the playwright James Barrie was in the theater with Dean. He watched the performance and left the theater without saying a word, but on his arrival home he wrote Dean "a eulogistic prophecy of the approaching night's events," on which, wrote Dean, "I look back . . . with some wistfulness, for, as I can remember it, he ended his letter by saying: 'Tonight you will have such a night in the theatre as never again in your life'."[41]

Barrie was perhaps a little too optimistic about *Hassan*'s success, for the press reviews after the first night were not unanimous in their praise. On the whole, they were favorable; and, though some critics remarked that the evening would have been intolerable without the spectacle, Flecker fared rather well, but Basil Dean did rather better. *The Times* review is typical. The writer admits that the spectacle has a rather confusing effect and that the play has an "intermittent" rather than "cumulative dramatic interest," but he states that not even *Chu Chin Chow* could compare "for artistic taste with the scenery of *Hassan*." *Chu Chin Chow*, he continues, "was entirely devoid of literary merit"; but *Hassan* "has not only a superb sense of style throughout, but frequently gushes forth in jets and rills of pure poetry."[42]

Other critics, however, were more inclined to praise Basil Dean at Flecker's expense. John Middleton Murry, who drew attention to *Hassan*'s lack of unity, stressed the spectacular effects of Dean's production. Reading Flecker's "Bayswatery Bagdad" play, wrote Murry, one finds "a confused pattern with threads of real beauty, an effort of a genuine poet to say something beyond his own immature capacity of utterance, and to say it in a form over which he had manifestly no control." The performance at His Majesty's, he continued, is a splendid production; "but the thing that is noticeably not produced is a play." The ballets were marvelous: "Never before," he wrote, "have I seen such a triumphant, Grundy-silencing combination of nudity and nobility"; the dancers looked like "angels on probation who had by mistake slipped off their wings with their underclothes." But, Murry concluded, though the spectacle is "lovely," and though *Hassan* "be produced to infinity, it cannot be produced into a play."[43]

When Herbert Farjeon drew attention to some of the play's deficiencies, he praised Dean's production. The poetry of *Hassan*, he wrote, is certainly fine; but the plot is disjointed and episodic; and the action slows perceptibly when Hassan half way through the play retires from the center of the stage. However, he concluded, the production was magnificent; Basil Dean had never done anything quite so excellently before.[44]

More recent critics of the play, though no longer dazzled and distracted by the spectacular effects of Dean's production, have not been able to agree about *Hassan*'s merit. Their opinions range from the cool dismissal of Allardyce Nicoll to the enthusiastic approval of George Wilson Knight. To Nicoll, the play is completely disorganized: "The ridiculous buffoonery of Hassan, the idealistic rapture of the poet Ishak, and the love-passion of the two forlorn figures whose tortured screams in the last act make the poem [sic] a patchwork of heterogeneous elements without harmony and without form."[45] To George Wilson Knight, *Hassan* is "one of those rare dramas which make an important epoch live."[46] Neither criticism is entirely just, and both Nicoll and Knight overstate their views. Nicoll, judging the play mainly in terms of its structure, finds it lacking in formal unity and dismisses it; Knight, who believes that it is the aim of drama "to make profitable terms with the alien powers surrounding man,"[47] views the play as an extended metaphor and, finding ample scope for symbolic interpretation, praises it more highly than it deserves.

Hassan, it is true, is not a unified play; the first half, in which Hassan and Yasmin are the center of interest, does not integrate with the second half, where attention is focused on the fate of Rafi and Pervaneh. The tone is uncertain, and one is never quite sure whether to view Hassan as a buffoon or as a sympathetic figure caught in events over which he has no control. But the play is far from being a graceless failure, nor is it merely a lavish but empty spectacle. On the contrary, it is a successful and at times moving expression of the dubious value of art, a theme which takes an added poignancy and depth in the light of Flecker's career.

The thematic center of the play are the two characters Hassan and Ishak; and the latter is described by Flecker in a letter to Frank Savery of July, 1913, as the "chief character."[48] In a sense, they represent, like James Joyce's Leopold Bloom and Stephen Daedalus in *Ulysses*, bumbling, commonplace humanity, and the cool, deliberate, detached artist. As in *Ulysses*, where Stephen after a series of adventures and misadventures with Mr. Bloom finally learns to accept, even admire, the ambiguous heroism of struggling humanity, Ishak learns in *Hassan* to accept, even to love, his weak, overweight confectioner friend, and therefore accompanies him at the end of the play on the "Golden Journey to Samarkand." It is almost as if Flecker, the Parnassian poet, had come to recognize, like Ishak, that, though being an artist is supposedly a fine thing, it is nothing unless coupled with an awareness of and affection for humanity.

This, however, is only part of the play's meaning; for Flecker also raises the question whether the artistic impulse is compatible with an interest in humanity, or whether the artist sees people and the world in which he lives as simply components of a potential artistic design. After all, the Caliph has the artistic instinct:

Have you not seen the designer of carpets, O Hassan of Bagdad, put here the blue and here the gold, here the orange and here the green? So have I seen the Caliph take the life of some helpless man — who was contented in his little house and garden, enjoying the blue of happy days — and colour his life with the purple of power, and streak it with the crimson of lust: then whelm it all in the gloom-greys of abasement, touched with the glaring reds of pain, and edge the whole with the black border of annihilation.[49]

Throughout the play, Flecker emphasizes the close relationship between esthetics and sadism; and one is forced to consider whether the artistic spirit is incompatible with a concern for humanity and is, in fact, openly hostile to it.

In Act V, for example, in "the Procession of Protracted Death," which calls for elaborately beautiful costumes and setting,[50] Flecker exemplifies the closeness between beauty and perverse cruelty; the Caliph takes an artistic delight in devising the poetic fate of Rafi and

Pervaneh; and the beautiful fountain designed by "a Greek of Constantinople" for Caliph El Madhi, Haroun-al-Raschid's father, has also sadistic associations since its creator had been executed after the fountain's completion to ensure that it would remain "the loveliest in the world."[51] In short, art which should be, in Hassan's words, "a deliverance from Hell," providing emotional and spiritual sustenance for humanity, has become at best "a princely diversion" that is valued for the immortality it can confer, or at worst a means of devising an elaborate Hell, such as that provided for Rafi and Pervaneh.[52] Thus art, popularly supposed to be a comfort for mankind, is something quite different; and its failure is perhaps to be attributed to the corrupt nature of man.

As Ishak says in response to Hassan's question about why be a poet if it means observing and recording the less pleasant aspects of life: "Allah did not ask me that question when he made me a poet and a dissector of souls. It is my trade: I do but follow my master, the exalted Designer of human carpets, the Ruler of the world. If he prepared the situation, shall I not observe the characters? Thus I corrupt my soul to create — Allah knoweth what — ten little words like rubies glimmering in a row."[53]

Realizing that the poet's vocation is not so noble as popularly supposed, and that the poet's spirit must become corrupted merely in the exercise of its powers, Ishak vows to relinquish his role as an artist and to become a pilgrim instead: "I am leaving this city of slaves, this Bagdad of fornication. I have broken my lute and will write no more qasidahs in praise of the generosity of kings. I will try the barren road and listen for the voice of the emptiness of the earth. And you [Hassan] shall walk beside me."[54] So Hassan, acknowledging this wisdom of Ishak's gesture, prepares to accompany him and to leave behind the magnificent Isfahan carpet the Caliph had given him, but to take with him instead his old, beautifully simple Bokhara which, says Ishak, he can stretch out on the desert when he says his evening prayer, "and it shall be a little meadow in the waste of sand."[55] When the two men leave on their pilgrimage "for lust of knowing what should not be known," they leave the women behind to lament that men "have their dreams," and think not of them; and the play closes with the words of the distant chorus: "We take the Golden Road to Samarkand."[56]

With a poet like Flecker, who wrote verse less from an urge to communicate his innermost thoughts and feelings than to "create . . . ten little words like rubies glimmering in a row," it is dangerous to read his work as a metaphor of his personal experience; but in the case of *Hassan*, Flecker's most important work, it is tempting to do so. Certainly, Flecker's poetic instinct had not brought him much happiness. Regarding the East with a poet's eye, he was drawn into a career for which he had little aptitude or sympathy; and, once in the Orient, his nostalgic, poetic vision of the Cotswolds and the Bournemouth pines made him restless and sick for home. One feels, too, that Flecker's marriage to Hellé Skiardaressi was motivated less by genuine feeling for the lady herself than by a poetic passion for Hellenistic civilization; and, though the marriage seems to have been tolerably successful, reading between the lines of his published correspondence in which his wife's name is hardly ever mentioned, one feels that it was far from ideal.[57] Could it be that Flecker was expressing in *Hassan* his own personal disillusionment, having realized that the dream world created by a poet's imagination and sublunar reality are two very different things? Certainly *Hassan* has something to say about what Dr. Johnson called "the dangerous prevalence of the imagination," and the next to last line in the play about men having their dreams and ignoring their women — to which one may add Hellé Flecker's choice of inscription for her husband's grave, "O Lord! Restore his realm to the dreamer" — all indicate that Flecker was aware of his obsessive tendency to create dreams even in the face of conflicting reality. Under these circumstances, the only alternative left to the poet is to seek a state beyond art — to take the "Golden Road to Samarkand."

Hassan is a successful play; and, though one hesitates to endorse George Wilson Knight's sweeping claim that "its sophisticated insight, exact patterning and extraordinary inclusiveness serve to sum up [the Edwardian] period, if not our tragic tradition,"[58] it is certainly more than a hollow, rather confusing spectacle. Closer to the truth is Priscilla Thouless' sensitive evaluation, which states that "[Flecker] clung to the Parnassian path because he feared self-expression; he feared that if he did not strictly confine himself he would turn to gross egoism, like that of Victor Hugo, or to didacticism like that of Wordsworth. He feared moreover that his 'healthy manliness' might fade away, and that his divided soul might be revealed. In *Hassan* it is revealed, for in *Hassan* we find the hand of the Parnassian and of the Romantic; we find an imperfect amalgam of different elements in a play, the texture of which is solid and brilliant."[59] Certainly Flecker's Parnassianism and his Romanticism are present in the play, but they are not in conflict. Flecker finds

Parnassianism too trivial and Romanticism dangerously misleading; consequently, he sees the only possibility of salvation in a nameless state beyond art. This insight, coming from a man prone to delude himself rather than face the truth, makes *Hassan* a satisfying play and, at the same time, makes Flecker's personality seem more sympathetic than it might otherwise have appeared.

CHAPTER 6

Conclusion

IN estimating the status of relatively minor writers, one is tempted to elevate their significance by claiming for them the role of "transitional figure," "important influence," "experimentalist," or any other such title which draws attention from their actual literary achievement and directs it instead toward their place in literary history. It is difficult, however, to resort to such tactics with Flecker; for, in so far as he is representative of a literary movement, he is a late Parnassian who strove to emulate the past achievements of such people as Henri de Régnier and Paul Fort when his contemporaries, T. S. Eliot and Ezra Pound, for example, had already made the transition from Parnassianism to Imagism. Flecker's work in poetry, prose, and drama is not especially original; and just about the only way he may be said to have influenced anyone was when his poem "The Queen's Song"[1] was brought to the attention of W. B. Yeats by T. Sturge Moore, thereby providing the Irish poet with the possible inspiration for "Byzantium," both poems dealing with the idea of living beauty as opposed to "changeless metal."[2]

At one time, Flecker was considered the leader of what Herbert Palmer referred to as "the first Georgian Revolt" — a poetical movement conceived in opposition to the kind of poetry written by such people as Rudyard Kipling and William Watson. He was also regarded as "one of the most powerful influences in the second" revolt which centered around reaction against John Masefield. Furthermore, said Palmer writing in 1938, "he might still become one of the most powerful influences against Modernist disintegration," meaning the "new" poetry sponsored by T. E. Hulme, Ezra Pound, and T. S. Eliot, whose *The Waste Land* Palmer regarded as an elaborate literary joke.[3] In fact, Flecker never became the center of any literary movement; and, though he regarded himself in the preface to *The Golden Journey to Samarkand* as a member of "the classical reaction . . . against sentimentality and extravagance,"[4] which in a very real sense he was, one could hardly call this literary reaction a "movement."

Although Flecker had his literary friends, notably Edward Marsh and Rupert Brooke, he, living abroad, had little opportunity to become involved with the gossip and skirmishing of the contemporary literary scene. Though he knew Harold Monro, proprietor of the Poetry Bookshop which was the operational headquarters of the Georgian movement, one finds no record of his attending the poetry readings and literary discussions held there.[5] As for the Modernists, he seems not to have understood them at all; he admitted in a letter to Harold Monro of March 22, 1914, that he liked Ezra Pound "as a joke," but he saw no point in taking him seriously. [6] Later in a letter to Edward Marsh of March 28, 1914, Flecker wrote facetiously of a "Projected futurist poem beginning: 'I slobber on the Parthenon'."[7] The kind of poet Flecker admired is the now forgotten Richard Middleton, whose poem "The Pirate Ship" almost certainly influenced Flecker's "The Old Ships,"[8] and to whom Flecker was determined to dedicate his next volume of verse after *The Golden Journey to Samarkand.*[9]

In short, Flecker has little claim to be considered as either influential or farsighted. He must be judged quite simply in terms of his work alone. Fortunately, having a profound respect for poetry as an art, he wrote carefully; and there is little in his poetry, prose, or drama that deserves to be ignored.[10] He had his lapses, but these were lapses of taste and artistic intelligence rather than carelessness; and, though much of his writing seems hardly relevant to our times, his work will never be entirely forgotten as long as careful literary craftsmanship is respected. It is true that he lacked what — for want of a better word — one may call "vision." It is also true that, except possibly in *Hassan*, he never really took himself seriously; but in that play at least he made a comment upon the nature of art which reveals a maturity of outlook never attained by, for example, his better known contemporary Rupert Brooke. This attainment suggests that, had Flecker been allowed the opportunity to develop, he might have become a more considerable figure than he is.

As Robert Lynd has written in an excellent, brief summary of Flecker's achievement, his genius "was founded in the love of literature more than in the love of life"; and, like his admired Théophile Gautier, "he was one of those for whom the visible world exists. But it existed for him less in nature than in art." Nevertheless, continues Lynd, "it is interesting to see how in some of his later work his imagination is feeling its way back from the world of illusion to the world of real things — from Bagdad and Babylon to England."[11] And in this change lies the tragedy, if one may call it that, of Flecker. He discovered the dangerous sterility of dreams, but his insight came too late. As he wrote in one of his finest poems, "The Old Ships":

> I have seen old ships sail like swans asleep
> Beyond the village which men call Tyre,
> With leaden age o'ercargoed, dipping deep
> For Famagusta and the hidden sun
> That rings black Cyprus with a lake of fire;
> And all those ships were certainly so old
> Who knows how oft with squat and noisy gun,
> Questing brown slaves or Syrian oranges,
> The pirate Genoese
> Hell-raked them till they rolled
> Blood, water fruit and corpses up to the hold.
> But now through friendly seas they softly run,
> Painted the mid-sea blue or shore-sea green,
> Still patterned with the vine and grapes in gold.

But, continues Flecker, he has also seen,

> Painting her shapely shadows from the dawn
> An image tumbled on a rose-swept bay,
> A drowsy ship of some yet older day;
> And, wonder's breath indrawn,
> Thought I — who knows — who knows — but in that same
> (Fished up beyond Aeaeam patched up new
> — Stern painted brighter blue —)
> That talkative, bald-headed seaman came
> (Twelve patient comrades sweating at the oar)
> From Troy's doom-crimson shore,
> And with great lies about his wooden horse
> Set the crew laughing, and forgot his course.

> It was so old a ship — who knows, who knows?
> — And yet so beautiful, I watched in vain
> To see the mast burst open with a rose,
> And the whole deck put on its leaves again.[12]

Flecker was a dilettante; he dabbled in literature much as he dabbled in diplomacy. In his poetry, in his prose, and in his drama one senses, on occasions, that he was trying to reach out beyond his preoccupation with self, to be something more than a cultivated man of letters, but these moments are rare. His play *Hassan* has earned him a permanent, though minor, place in the history of modern drama, and the continued anthologizing of such poems as "Tenebris Interlucentem," "A Ship, an Isle, a Sickle Moon," and "Town Without a Market" has ensured that his poetical talents are not forgotten. Nevertheless, he remains an indisputably minor figure.

Just as his vanity, complacency, and insensitivity to the feelings of others rendered him incapable of being either a sympathetic husband or an effective member of the foreign service, so these defects of character seem to have inhibited his development as a writer. He remained, almost to the end, the typical Edwardian gentleman. Meanwhile, to paraphrase the memorable words of British Foreign Secretary Sir Edward Grey, "the lights had gone out all over Europe," and his gloomy prediction that there was little chance of their being lit again soon never seemed more likely than it did on August 3, 1914, when he stood up in the House of Commons to prepare the country for World War I. For England, as for Flecker, the time for dreams was over. It was the end of an era, and Flecker's death was a symbol of its passing.

Notes and References

Preface

1. John Heath-Stubbs, F. T. Prince, Stephen Spender, *Penguin Modern Poets 20* (Harmondsworth, Middlesex, 1971), p. 54.
   2. Geraldine Hodgson, *James Elroy Flecker* (Oxford, 1925), p. 225.
   3. *Collected Prose* (London, 1922), pp. 246 - 247.

Chapter One

1. Charles Williams, *Flecker of Dean Close* (London: Canterbury Press, 1946), p. 43.
   2. *Ibid.*, p. 59.
   3. Hodgson, p. 18.
   4. T. Stanley Mercer, *James Elroy Flecker: From School to Samarkand* (Thames Ditton, Surrey, 1952), pp. 7 - 8.
   5. In her biography of Flecker, Geraldine Hodgson prints an example of the poet's early verse, an extract from a piece entitled "The Story of Christopher," which contains the following lines (p. 25):

> Let days of Joy, let days of Grief slip by,
> Of old regrets muse not, nor coming care.
> When trouble heavy on thy heart doth lie,
> When thou art prospering forget not prayer.
>
> Then on thy soul shall come the perfect peace
> And midst thy toil a respite and a rest.
> Joy shall be thine till weary work doth cease
> And thou shalt reign above for ever blest.

6. Mercer, p. 10.
   7. Hodgson, pp. 48 - 50.
   8. *Ibid.*, p. 61.

9. *Ibid.*, p. 62.

10. For a more detailed discussion of 1890s Estheticism and Decadence, see Karl Beckson's introduction to *Aesthetes and Decadents of the 1890s* (New York: Vintage Books, 1967).

11. Douglas Goldring, *James Elroy Flecker* (London, 1922), pp. 12 - 13.

12. *Ibid.*, p. 15.

13. Hodgson, p. 68.

14. *Ibid.*, p. 72.

15. *Ibid.*

16. *Ibid.*, p. 91.

17. Humbert Wolfe, "James Elroy Flecker and the Red Man" in *Portraits By Inference* (London, 1934), pp. 10 - 12.

18. Clerihew is the name given to a quatrain of light verse characterized by two couplets of irregular meter which poke fun at a particular well-known person, whose name forms one of the rhymes. It was invented by Edmund Clerihew Bentley who, supposedly while listening at school to a chemistry lecture, wrote:

> Sir Humphry Davy
> Abominated gravy.
> He lived in the odium
> Of having discovered sodium.

19. *The Best Man* (Oxford, Eights Week, 1906), p. 3.

20. John Sherwood, *No Golden Journey* (London, 1973), p. 34.

21. *Collected Poems*, (London, 1946), p. 133.

22. Hodgson, p. 66.

23. *Ibid.*, p. 46.

24. *Ibid.*, pp. 48 - 50.

25. *Ibid.*, p. 79.

26. *Ibid.*, pp. 107 - 08.

27. *Ibid.*, p. 110.

28. Goldring, p. 29.

29. *Ibid.*, pp. 51 - 52.

30. Goldring may have been confused about the date of the Bordeaux incident, as elsewhere, describing Flecker's Cambridge years, he recalls a trip Flecker made to the South of France "at the time of the great wine troubles" in the company of J. J. Knox, a student-interpreter who was later posted to Teheran. They found themselves in trouble in a small town and, according to Flecker's account of the incident, "were only saved from the mob through the Mayor's belief that they were spies: he rescued them, and smuggled them away from the station by holding up an express, in order [as Flecker believed] to put the Government under an obligation [the revolt was then already near collapse]." (Goldring, pp. 35 - 36.)

31. Hodgson, p. 113.

32. *Ibid.*, pp. 123 - 24.

33. *Ibid.*

34. Christopher Hassall, *Rupert Brooke* (London, 1964), p. 107. There is a fuller portrait of Oscar Browning in Desmond MacCarthy, *Portraits* (London: Putnam, 1955), pp. 34 - 38.

35. See A. J. A. Symons, *The Quest For Corvo* (Harmondsworth, Middlesex; Penguin, 1966), pp. 203 - 06.

36. Sherwood, p. xvii.

37. Goldring, pp. 21 - 22.

38. *Ibid.*, p. 34.

39. Hodgson, p. 135.

40. Mercer, p. 27.

41. Shane Leslie, *The Cantab* (London, 1926), *passim*.

42. See Hassall, pp. 118 - 19.

43. In his critical biography of Brooke, Hassall quotes part of a letter from Brooke to James Strachey: "Lunch with Flecker today was simply Hellish — old cold bloaters, sardine paste, and the relics of your gooseberries — oh, and dirty! hairs in the butter! soot in the cream! Why does he creep so!" (*Ibid.*, p. 188.) In April, 1912, however, Brooke wrote to Flecker: "My swarthy friend, Elroy, my golden-tongued and lax-metred Orpheus, you would never let me teach you how to write Poetry, but it does not matter now: and you are a fine fellow." (*Some Letters From Abroad*, ed. Hellé Flecker [London, 1930], p. 17.)

44. Hassall, p. 192.

45. Hodgson, p. 137.

46. *Ibid.*, p. 142.

47. Some of the poems which Flecker wrote during his years at Cambridge were used to supplement *The Bridge of Fire*, which was revised and reissued as *Thirty-Six Poems* shortly before he left Cambridge. The following pieces he contributed to *The Cambridge Review* while he was at the university: "The Parrot" (November 4, 1909, p. 70); "From the Gulistan of Sa'di" (November 25, 1909, p. 137); "Mansur" (January 20, 1910, pp. 202 - 03); "More Gulistan" (February 24, 1910, pp. 294 - 95); "Pentheus" (May 26, 1910, p. 434).

48. Hodgson, p. 146.

49. Writing to his mother in late 1913 about his brother Oswald, he said: "Don't let Oswald go to Cambridge, Clare, Selwyn, the Hall. He might as well join a baby club. Oxford is a much better place for him. There he can be intelligent without becoming a freak. Will write very seriously *re* worthlessness of almost all Cambridge colleges if you like." (Hodgson, p. 219.)

Chapter Two

1. Marzieh Gail, *Persia and the Victorians* (London: Allen and Unwin, 1951), p. 36.

2. Frank Harris, *Contemporary Portraits* (New York: Harrap, 1915), pp. 187 - 90.

3. See Amy Cruse, *The Victorians and Their Reading* (London: Allen and Unwin, 1935), pp. 286, 291 - 92. See also Margaret Cecilia Annam, "The Arabian Nights in Victoria Literature," unpublished Ph.D. dissertation, Northwestern University, 1945.

4. Elizabeth Monroe, *Britain's Moment in the Middle East: 1914 - 1956* (London: Weidenfeld and Nicolson, 1963), pp. 11 - 14.

5. Hodgson, p. 95.

6. *Ibid.*, p. 88.

7. *Ibid.*, p. 256.

8. *Ibid.*, p. 83.

9. Monroe, p. 15.

10. "Candilli," *Collected Prose*, p. 158.

11. *Ibid.*

12. "The Bus in 'Stambul," *Collected Prose*, pp. 61 - 62.

13. Sir Reader Bullard broadcast some of his reminiscences of Flecker on the British Broadcasting Company, his talk being published in *The Listener* on February 15, 1951, pp. 268 - 69.

14. Hodgson, p. 161.

15. Sherwood, p. 113.

16. Hodgson, p. 168.

17. Godfrey Elton, "James Elroy Flecker," in *Dictionary of National Biography, 1912 - 1921*, ed. H. W. C. Davis and J. R. H. Weaver (London: Oxford University Press, 1927), p. 189.

18. *Some Letters From Abroad*, p. 30.

19. See *ibid.*, p. 55. T. E. Lawrence, who was staying in the hotel at the same time, also describes the incident in *An Essay on Flecker* (London, 1937), p. 2.

20. *Some Letters From Abroad*.

21. *Ibid.*, p. 53.

22. "Forgotten Warfare," *Collected Prose*, pp. 72 - 74.

23. It is interesting to compare Flecker's account of the bombardment with those of Consul General R. A. Cumberbatch and Edmund Atiyah, the Lebanese writer, scholar, and diplomat. Flecker's account differs in no important respect from the official report, but the tone of Atiyah's description is in sharp contrast to the detached irony of Flecker's:

Enclosure 2 in No. 108.
Consul-General Cumberbatch to Sir G. Lowther.

(No. 12.)   Beirout, February 29, 1912.

Sir,
/With reference to my despatch No. 11 of yesterday's date on the subject of the destruction of the Turkish gun-boat and torpedo-boat/, I have the honour to report as

follows on the perturbation caused in this town by the action of the Italian war-ships.

Ever since the panic caused in the autumn by the false report as to the intentions of the Italian forces to effect a landing at Beirout, /as described in my despatch No. 65 of the 9th November, 1911/, there has existed a certain unrest due to the feeling that the possibility of such an event was not past, so that the mere sight of the Italian ships off the town on the 24th immediately created a panic among the inhabitants. The Moslems, with visions of the sufferings of their co-religionaries in Tripoli, feared for themselves, and a general exodus of their women and children to the Lebanon took place, whilst the men rushed in great numbers to the barracks and demanded arms, which, being refused, they overpowered the sentinels and broke into the "Redif" depot, carrying away 1,080 rifles and the contents of 90 cases cartridges. Some returned to their quarter of the town, whilst others joined the crowd, all armed, on the quays of the harbour.

Others broke into two or three shops where sporting rifles and guns were sold and took all they could, besides looting them of their other goods.

It was during these first moments of excitement that three or four Christians and one Russian Jew, mistaken for Italians, were killed, and foreigners found in the streets were hustled and menaced. One Druze was killed and another wounded for refusing to join a party of Moslems and "go for" the foreigners.

Mr. Acting Vice-Consul Flecker, who was driving back from the consulate-general to his hotel to bring Mrs. Flecker to the consulate-general at about 9 A.M. with a "cavass" and accompanied by M. Tchelkovnikof, Russian consul of Hama, was stopped by a menacing crowd near the barracks, and owed his escape from further possible violence to the timely intervention of a soldier and an armed civilian, who saw him and his companion safely to their hotel. (Appreciation of the conduct of this soldier has been duly expressed to the authorities.)

The Christians all fled from their offices and shops in the business quarter to their houses in justifiable fear of the rabble.

In the meantime, the Governor-General, Hazim Bey, assisted by the military commandant-general, Hashim Pasha, and the gendarmerie commandant, Colonel Nasmi Bey, took prompt and effectual measures to prevent the molestation of foreigners and Christians by the armed Moslem mob and to defend the Government House against a rush on the central prison in the ground-floor.

When I went at 10 A.M. to see Hazim Bey, whom I found at the police station surrounded by all the authorities and an excited Moslem mob clamouring for the evacuation of the prisoners, I found that he had the Moslem mob in hand, and I drove round to the various British institutions and to some British families to reassure them as to the situation, but recommending them to stay indoors that day and the next. I sent similar messages to the Christian quarter in which this consulate-general is situated.

At my request, the Governor-General had immediately placed strong military guards at the consulates, principal hotels (to which many Italians afterwards fled), and some foreign institutions, banks, &c., owing to the unmistakable intention shown by the Moslem crowd to revenge themselves on foreigners.

/At the police station I was shown several dead bodies, of which one was that of a' woman, and I passed several being carried in the streets which were deserted by Christians but filled with Moslems carrying military rifles and every species of firearms and swords, which state of things continued all that day and night.

On Sunday the arrival of three squadrons of the 30th Cavalry Regiment from Damascus, followed by two squadrons of the 28th and 29th Regiments, strengthened the hands of the authorities in tackling the mob, who resisted their attempts to get back the stolen rifles, and martial law was proclaimed. On Monday orders came from Constantinople to mobilise such "redifs" as the general might consider necessary, but he had mobilised only the Beirout battalion. Over 1,000 men presented themselves within 24 hours, showing keenness to be enrolled; but the Governor-General thinks that their services can be dispensed with now.

As stated in my telegram No. 8 of the 26th, Hazim Bey, the Governor-General, deserves commendation for the courage and energy displayed by him in extremely difficult circumstances, and it is universally recognised that it was due to the prompt measures taken by him with the assistance of General Hashim Pasha, Colonel Nazmi Bey, of the gendarmerie, and Husni Bey, chief of police, that graver disorders were prevented. His Excellency, after being faced with the serious and pressing question of the surrender of his country's war-ships, followed by their destruction, had to deal immediately with the armed rabble menacing the prisons and the necessity of safeguarding the threatened lives and property of foreigners and Christians. Most of the time he went about on foot unprotected by an escort, as all vehicles had gone away with refuges, and all the military gendarmerie and police forces were employed in different parts of the town.

According to the reports of the vice-consuls under my superintendence the news of the events at Beirout, which were exagerated into a bombardment of the town and a landing of troops, created a great stir owing to a fear that similar action might be taken at other ports on this coast, but the authorities acted with due promptitude, and as true versions of what took place came to hand the excitement calmed down.

At Fourni Chubak, a Lebanese frontier guard-house, an affray took place between the guard of thirty men and one or two score Moslems fleeing into the mountain, most of them carrying rifles taken from the Beirout redif depot, which the Lebanese officer insisted upon being given up to him. The crowd would not yield and preferred returning to the town. There were three or four casualties.

I have, &c.

H. A. CUMBERBATCH.
(Reprinted from official documents at the British Embassy, Beirut).

o   o   o   o

When the Turko-Italian War broke out in 1911, my mother and I were again living with my grandfather in Beyrouth. The sympathies of the Christian Syrians were entirely on the Italian side. I was then just old enough to take notice of such an event, and from what I heard came to take a keen interest in it. Our detested sovereign Turkey was at war with a Christian power, and naturally I wanted the Christian power to win. I would sit and listen to the war news being discussed in privacy (for no one dared discuss it in public) by my grandfather and his friends, and exalt over the defeat of the Turks. And then occurred the most exciting event in my young life — an event which at once appealed to my sense of adventure, and filled me with the utmost thrills of triumphant joy.

An Italian naval squadron came to Beyrouth in the course of the war, and after a short bombardment sank two Turkish destroyers at anchor in Beyrouth harbour. It was a day in early February. The Italian cruisers were sighted on the horizon at dawn, and the news rapidly spread over the city. I happened to go out of the house after breakfast, on an errand to the grocer's, and soon gathered that there was something unusual in the air. There was a stir and a hum in the street. People who should have been at their work in the town were coming back, walking hurriedly, as if trying to

reach their houses before something happened. Some of these stopped for a second here and there to impart hurried information to a friend or acquaintance whom they chanced to meet proceeding on his normal way. Shopkeepers were standing outside their shops, communing quietly with one another, stopping new arrivals from the town to ask questions in an undertone. Some of them who had just opened their shops were closing them again, turning customers away. On everybody's face there was an expression of suppressed excitement, of fearful anticipation. At the grocer's shop I heard one or two words from which I began to understand what was happening, or about to happen. I hurried back home and at the gate met my grandfather, who had been out too and brought with him definite news. An Italian fleet was coming to bombard the Turkish boats in the harbour. It was not likely that the town would be molested, unless the land batteries were to fire at the Italians. In any case the safest thing for us to do was to go to the British School, where we should be under protection of the Union Jack. My grandfather had seen the Headmistress, and she had told him that she had received instructions from the British Consul to hoist the flag over the school, in case the Italians were to bombard the town.
(Edward Atiyah, *An Arab Tells His Story* (London: John Murray, 1946), reprinted in Arnold Hottinger, *The Arabs* (London: Thames and Hudson, 1963), pp. 211 - 13.

24. "Forgotten Warfare," *Collected Prose*, pp. 69 - 71.

25. Lawrence, p. 2.

26. Writing to Frank Savery in July, 1913, Flecker exclaimed: "I loathe the East and Easterners. . . . Yet it seems — even to hardened Orientalists — that I understand." (*Some Letters From Abroad*, p. 98.)

27. Hodgson, pp. 171 - 72.

28. From 1941 to 1944, Durrell was foreign press service officer in the British Information Office, Cairo, and press attaché at Alexandria from 1944 to 1945. His experiences here and at other quasi-diplomatic posts he held during his career are described in his best-known work, the four-part novel *The Alexandria Quartet* (London: Faber and Faber, 1957 - 60), and in *Esprit de Corps: Sketches From Diplomatic Life* (London: Faber and Faber, 1957).

29. A recent issue of the supplement to the Arabic newspaper *An-Nahar* (January 14, 1968, pp. 16 - 17) contains the text of an interview with Mrs. Farida Al'Akl, who, besides knowing Flecker, also taught T. E. Lawrence Arabic. Mention is made in the article of Flecker's bad temper and of his propensity for taking walks, especially to the tomb, where he supposedly composed much of his verse.

30. See Lawrence's letter to Flecker of June, 1914, from Karcamesh concerning a minor affray there, in *The Letters of T. E. Lawrence*, ed. David Garnett, with a foreword by Capt. B. G. Liddell Hart. (London: Spring Books, 1964), p. 171.

31. Writing to his mother from Karcamesh on June 24, 1911, Lawrence had said: "Fortunately there is no foreign influence as yet in the district: if only you had seen the ruination caused by the French influence, and to a lesser degree by the American, you would never wish it extended. The

perfectly hopeless vulgarity of the half-Europeanised Arab is appalling. Better a thousand times the Arab untouched. The foreigners come out here always to teach, whereas they had much better learn, for in everything but wits and knowledge the Arab is generally the better man of the two." (*The Diary of T. E. Lawrence* [London, 1937]. A privately printed pamphlet, of which only 203 copies were published; no pagination.]

32. *Ibid.*

33. Besides being a prominent figure in the contemporary literary scene, editing the *Georgian Poetry* anthologies from 1912 to 1921, Edward Marsh (1872 - 1953) was also a man of considerable influence and power. As private secretary to a number of prominent British statesmen — notably Joseph Chamberlain, Herbert Asquith, and Winston Churchill — Marsh established personal contacts which enabled him to dispense a limited degree of patronage.

34. Christopher Hassall, *Edward Marsh: Patron of the Arts* (London, 1959), p. 200.

35. *Ibid.*

36. *Ibid.*, p. 201.

37. Public Records Office, FO 369/518.

38. *Ibid.*

39. Hodgson, p. 183.

40. *Ibid.*, p. 184.

41. *Ibid.*

42. *Collected Poems*, p. 182.

43. *Ibid.*, p. 194.

44. Rupert Brooke, *1914 and Other Poems* (London: Sidgwick and Jackson, 1915), pp. 59 - 63.

45. *Collected Poems*, p. 179.

46. See Hodgson, p. 188.

47. *Ibid.*, p. 191.

48. Goldring, p. 104.

49. Hodgson, pp. 218 - 19.

50. *Ibid.*, p. 223.

51. *Ibid.*, p. 221.

52. Brooke, p. 15.

53. *Collected Poems*, p. 225.

Chapter Three

1. *Georgian Poetry*, ed. James Reeves (Harmondsworth, Middlesex: Penguin, 1962).

2. Robert Ross, *The Georgian Revolt* (Carbondale, Illinois: University of Southern Illinois Press, 1967), p. 115.

3. See *Collected Poems*, pp. 48, 179. It is perhaps worth noting that

Flecker himself felt he was "horribly unGeorgian." (*Some Letters From Abroad*, p. 153.)

4. See *Aesthetes and Decadents of the 1890s*, p. xix.

5. See *ibid.*, pp. xvii - xl. For a more detailed discussion of English Parnassianism see James K. Robinson, "A Neglected Phase of the Aesthetic Movement: English Parnassianism," *PMLA*, LXVIII (1953), 733 - 54; Frank M. Tierney, "Edmund Gosse and the Revival of French Mixed Forms," *English Literature in Transition*, XIV (1971), 191 - 99; John M. Munro, "Introduction," *Selected Poems of Theo Marzials* (Beirut: A. U. B. 1974), *passim*.

6. Elton, p. 189.

7. "Putting his observations of Camden Town into old stanzas, and on the Bosporous wishing in prose that he might be invigorated by the sight of a London gasometer, but never finding a form to say it in verse," Flecker was, writes Howarth, something of a failure. (*Notes on Some Figures Behind T. S. Eliot* [London: Chatto and Windus, 1964], p. 108.)

8. Hodgson, p. 16.

9. *The Bridge of Fire* (London, 1907), p. 2

10. *Ibid.*, p. 18.

11. *Ibid.*, p. 39.

12. *Ibid.*, p. 46.

13. *Ibid.*, pp. 49, 27.

14. *Ibid.*, p. 61.

15. *Ibid.*, p. 29.

16. *Ibid.*, p. 49.

17. *Ibid.*, p. 48.

18. *Collected Poems*, p. 36.

19. "Introduction," *Collected Poems*, pp. xxi - xxiii.

20. *Ibid.*, p. 33.

21. Review of *The Bridge of Fire*, *Academy*, LXXIII (October 19, 1907), 33 - 34.

22. *Academy*, LXXIII (November 9, 1907), 124.

23. Goldring, p. 186.

24. *Collected Poems*, p. 65.

25. *Ibid.*, p. 98.

26. *Ibid.*, p. 91. Flecker is here taking an extreme position, suggesting that the artist who expects his creations to live on after him is guilty of vanity. Everything, even the products of the artistic imagination, are doomed to perish; therefore, it is the actual process of creation that is valuable, not what the artist creates. Arthur Symons, a writer and critic whom Flecker seems to have admired — he reviewed his *Romantic Movement in English Poetry* favorably for *The English Review* in February, 1911 (see pp. 00 - 00) — makes a similar point. Symons suggests that there is no essential difference in merit between the creation of a performer (the pianist, for example) and

an artist (the composer, for example, whose work the musician plays).
Indeed, because the artist wishes to perpetuate something of himself in his
creations, while the production of the performer dies the moment it is
created, the former may be said to be more egocentric, more selfish, and
therefore less pure an artist. What is important is the act of creation itself,
the value of which may only be judged in terms of its "beauty." (See *Plays,
Acting and Music* [London: Constable, 1909], pp. 321 - 22.)

27. *Collected Poems*, p. 75.

28. *Collected Prose*, p. 222.

29. *Ibid.*, pp. 207 - 14. Flecker has an earlier essay on Davidson as well,
written while he was at Oxford (see pp. 189 - 206.)

30. *Collected Poems*, pp. 79, 100.

31. The six poems added were: "Pillage," "The Ballad of Zacho,"
"Pavlovna in London," "The Sentimentalist," "Don Juan in Hell," and
"The Ballad of Iskandar." (See *Collected Poems*, pp. 126, 128, 133, 135,
137.)

32. *Collected Prose*, pp. 237 - 41.

33. It is impossible not to catch the personal note here. Surely Flecker also
had his father in mind? Dr. Flecker never appreciated his son's literary
achievements, and though while Flecker was alive, especially during the
later stages of his illness, he was as generous and considerate as any father
could have been, he could not come to terms with his poetry, mainly, one
feels, because it lacked moral seriousness and "message." (See Mercer, pp.
39 - 42).

34. Hodgson, pp. 200 - 02.

35. *Collected Poems*, p. 144.

36. *Ibid.*, p. 175.

37. *Letters of James Elroy Flecker to Frank Savery* (London, 1926),
p. 114.

38. *Collected Poems*, p. 176.

39. *Some Letters From Abroad*, p. 99. Flecker was always apt to hide his
less appealing traits behind his supposed good humor. Consider his poem
"Taoping," (*Collected Poems*, p. 196), reportedly suggested by "a strange
amazing book of one Daguerches, called *Consolata Fille du Soleil*' (*Some
Letters From Abroad*, p. 100), which deals with flagellation. About this
poem Flecker wrote to his wife: "Don't you think the healthy honest way for
a European to look at a Chinaman or a nigger is to laugh at him? Don't you
think they are there for the joy of the picturesque — as I portray them in
'Taoping'." (*Ibid.*)

40. The best brief discussion of French Symbolism is probably C. M.
Bowra, *The Heritage of Symbolism* (London: Macmillan, 1943), pp. 1 - 16.
For a more extensive, authoritative treatment, see A. G. Lehmann, *The
Symbolist Aesthetic in France: 1885 - 1895* (Oxford: Blackwell, 1950).

41. *Some Letters From Abroad*, p. 98.

42. *Collected Poems*, p. 232.

43. Hellé Flecker described the occasion in her collection of her husband's correspondence (*Some Letters From Abroad*, p. 35):

It is now deserted, the pilgrims proceeding by steamer and train, and the numerous khans that were grouped in that quarter are crumbling to ruins. We left the carriage and advanced on foot along the desolate Kaldcrin, the mud coming up nearly to the knees. On both sides as far as the eye could reach, the muddy track was bordered with rows and rows of thickly set tombs of pilgrims who had fallen on the way, behind them the immensity of the desert spread under a low, lead-coloured sky. Not a shrub or a blade of grass, the grey tombstones were crazily aslant in all directions, the stone turbans and fezes crowning them seemed stooping in crowded confusion and whispering old forgotten tales in the wind. The grandeur and desolation made us shudder, and we hurried back to the carriage with the night and terrror at our heels.

44. *Collected Poems*, pp. 151 - 59.
45. *Ibid.*, p. 210.
46. Hodgson, p. 167.
47. See Chapter 2, pp. 44 - 45.
48. *Letters to Frank Savery*, p. 56. In another letter to Savery, Flecker described Fort as a "joyish boyish Chesterton person," and he repeatedly enjoined his correspondent to read him. (*Some Letters From Abroad*, pp. 92, 110, 111, 115, 116, 119.)
49. *Collected Prose*, pp. 251 - 69.
50. *Collected Poems*, p. 226.
51. *Ibid.*, pp. 224, 225, 218, 223.
52. *Times Literary Supplement*, September 28, 1916, pp. 457 - 58.
53. *Letters to Frank Savery*, p. 131.
54. *Collected Poems*, pp. 198 - 209. In a letter to Frank Savery, Flecker wrote: "Gilbert Murray has written me a warm encomium of my Virgil translation which he, like me, considers the best ever made." (*Some Letters From Abroad*, p. 144.)
55. *Collected Poems*, pp. 236 - 38.
56. *Ibid.*, pp. 234 - 35. Flecker was an admirer of Kipling, and the lines

> Thou in his suppliant hands
> Hast placed such Mighty Lands:
> Save thou our King!
> As once from golden Skies
> Rebels with flaming eyes
> So the king's Enemies
> Doom Thou and Fling!

perhaps owe something to Kipling's poem "Recessional," which also expresses patriotic sentiments in a somewhat ambiguous way. Flecker himself was unsure about what he had written, commenting in a letter to Edward Marsh: "I can't make up my mind if it's rather good or a joke or both." (*Some Letters From Abroad*, p. 103.) Later the poet decided that his "Anthem" was in fact a "failure." (*Ibid.*, p. 145.)

57. *Collected Poems*, pp. 240 - 41.

Chapter Four

1. *Collected Prose.* pp. 189 - 205.
2. *Ibid.*, pp. 207 - 13.
3. *Ibid.*, pp. 215 - 28.
4. *Ibid.*, pp. 229 - 36.
5. *Ibid.*, pp. 243 - 50.
6. *Ibid.*, pp. 246 - 47.
7. *Ibid.*, pp. 249 - 50.
8. *Ibid.*, p. 22.
9. *Ibid.*, p. 25.
10. *Ibid.*, p. 26.
11. *Ibid.*, p. 32.
12. Flecker thought highly of *Degeneration*, calling it "a splendid work" though "mistaken in parts" and finding it "a wholesome antidote to much of the prevalent fin-de-siècle nonsense." (Hodgson, pp. 89 - 90.)
13. *Ibid.*, p. 89.
14. *Collected Prose*, pp. 33 - 38.
15. *Ibid.*, pp. 39 - 46.
16. *Letters to Frank Savery*, p. 178.
17. *The Bacchae of Euripides*, translated into English by G. G. A. Murray (London: Heath, 1904).
18. Sir Reader Bullard, "James Elroy Flecker in Constantinople," *The Listener*, February 15, 1951, pp. 268 - 69.
19. *The Scholars' Italian Book* (London, 1911), pp. v - viii.
20. Hodgson, p. 113.
21. *Collected Prose*, p. 153. Although *The Grecians* was published as a separate volume by J. M. Dent in 1910, it is also included in *Collected Prose*. For the sake of convenience, all references to this work are taken from *Collected Prose*. Cf. Walter Pater *The Renaissance* (London: Macmillan, 1910), pp. 237 - 38: "Philosophical theories or ideas, as points of view, instruments of criticism, may help us gather up what might otherwise pass unregarded by us, [but] the theory or idea or system which requires of us the sacrifice of any part of this experience, in consideration of some interest into which we cannot enter, or some abstract theory we have not identified with ourselves, or of what is only conventional, has no real claim on us. . . . [What we should aim at is] getting as many pulsations as possible into the given time, [striving for] a quickened sense of life."
22. *Collected Prose*, p. 144.

23. *Ibid.*, p. 146.
24. Ibid., p. 149.
25. *Ibid.*, p. 160.
26. *Ibid.*, p. 165.
27. *Ibid.*, pp. 167 - 68.
28. *Ibid.*, pp. 168 - 69.
29. *Ibid.*
30. *Ibid.*, p. 170.
31. *Ibid.*, pp. 171 - 77.
32. *Ibid.*, pp. 121 - 31.
33. Goldring, p. 155.
34. *Collected Prose*, p. 98.
35. *Ibid.*, p. 99.
36. Hodgson, p. 204.
37. Goldring, p. 54.
38. *Ibid.*, p. 89.
39. *Some Letters From Abroad*, p. 180.
40. *Letters to Frank Savery*, p. 183.
41. *Some Letters From Abroad*, p. 9.
42. *Ibid.*, p. 37.
43. *Ibid.*, p. 41.
44. *Ibid.*, p. 51.
45. *Ibid.*, p. 63.
46. Goldring, p. 86.
47. *Ibid.*, p. 88.
48. *The King of Alsander* (London, 1915), pp. 8 - 9.
49. Cf. *The King of Alsander*, pp. 143 ff. and Hellé Flecker's description of the British consul at Damascus in *Some Letters From Abroad*, pp. 33 - 34.
50. *The King of Alsander*, p. 10.
51. *Ibid.*, p. 16.
52. *Ibid.*, p. 102.
53. *Collected Poems*, pp. 196 - 97.
54. *Hassan*, pp. 164 - 65.
55. *Collected Prose*, pp. 130 - 31.
56. *The King of Alsander*, p. 133.
57. *Ibid.*, p. 134.
58. Lawrence, p. 4.
59. Sherwood, p. 132.
60. *The King of Alsander*, pp. 14 - 15.

Chapter Five

1. T. S. Eliot, "Poetry and Drama" in *Selected Prose*, ed. John Hayward (Harmondsworth, Middlesex: Penguin, 1953), pp. 85 - 86.
2. *The Wheel of Fire* (London, 1956), p. 16.

3. *Samhain* (Dublin), October, 1901, p. 61.

4. Max Beerbohm, *Seven Men* (London: Heinemann, 1919), pp. 185 - 218.

5. I.e. Stephen Phillips' *Nero*, Parts I and II; *Palicio*; *The Return of Ulysses*; *The Christian Captives*; *Achilles in Scyros*; *The Humours of the Court*; *The Feast of Bacchus*, all published between 1885 and 1893.

6. Note what Israel Zangwill said more than fifty years ago: "By his hasty seizure of current matter the poet loses the immense cooperation of the mytho-poetic instinct which shapes and selects the story, and of time, which invests it with glamour." ("Poetic Drama and the War," *The Poetry Review*, II [1916], 31 - 32.)

7. *Don Juan*, (London, 1925), pp. 12 - 19. Though Shakespeare's *Tempest* seems to have been in Flecker's mind in writing this scene, the actual source was certainly *Don Juan ou le festin de Pierre*, which contains a description of Don Juan's shipwreck and provides some hints for the character of Tisbea. (See Sherwood, p. 117, n. 2.)

8. *Collected Poems*, p. 135.

9. *Ibid.*, p. 189.

10. *Don Juan*, p. v.

11. *Ibid.*, p. vi.

12. Flecker's review of Monypenny's biography was published in *The Cambridge Review*, March 9, 1911, p. 350.

13. *Don Juan*, pp. 82 - 95.

14. *Ibid.*, p. ix.

15. Hodgson, p. 133.

16. Cf. Lord Framlingham's: "Entreat the forces of history, Juan; ask time why the world turns round. Can you arrest events, or tamper with the pre-ordained?" (*Don Juan*, p. 90), and Undershaft's: "Dare you make war on war?" (*The Complete Plays of George Bernard Shaw*, (London: Spring Books, 1965), p. 501.

17. *Some Letters From Abroad*, p. 41.

18. *Ibid.*, p. 44.

19. *Ibid.*, pp. 49 - 50.

20. *Don Juan*, p. viii.

21. John Davidson, *The Triumph of Mammon* (London: Grant Richards, 1907), pp. 152 - 53.

22. John Davidson, *Plays* (London: The Bodley Head, 1894), p. 251.

23. What may have encouraged Flecker's interest in this farcical tale is its partial similarity to St. John Wells Lucas-Lucas' prose fantasy *The Marble Sphinx* (London: Elkin Matthews, 1906), which was much in vogue while Flecker was at Cambridge. It deals with the love affair between a "corpulent man with a flushed and hideous face and a bald head" and "a pale girl with lips of startling scarlet and strange painted eyelids," the theme of the novel being beauty corrupted and humiliated by the passage of time. Whether or not Flecker was conscious of *The Marble Sphinx* when he was translating the

Turkish farce, it seems likely that at some stage of the composition of *Hassan* he had it in mind, for there are certain similarities between Lucas-Lucas' prose fantasy and the love affair between Yasmin and Hassan. (See Hassall, *Rupert Brooke*, pp. 130 - 32.)

24. See also *Collected Poems*, p. 158.

25. Details of the genesis and development of Flecker's play taken from Hellé Flecker's introduction to *Hassan* (London, 1922).

26. *Some Letters From Abroad*, p. 82.

27. Hassall, *Edward Marsh*, p. 205.

28. *Ibid.*, p. 245.

29. *Ibid.*, p. 206.

30. *Ibid.*, p. 246.

31. *Ibid.*, p. 265.

32. *Hassan* (acting version), ed. Basil Dean (London, 1951), p. xiv.

33. *Hassan* (London, 1922), pp. 10 - 11.

34. *Letters to Frank Savery*, p. 107.

35. *Some Letters From Abroad*, p. 134.

36. *Ibid.*, p. 152.

37. *Hassan* (acting version), p. xxii.

38. *The Oxford Book of Modern Verse: 1892 - 1935* (London: Oxford University Press, 1936), p. 1.

39. *Hassan*, p. 26.

40. It is worth noting that when *Hassan* was revived in 1951 at the Cambridge Theatre, London, it was a failure, the director having chosen to stage it in a deliberately simple style.

41. *Hassan* (acting version), p. xx.

42. *The Times* (London), September 21, 1923, p. 8.

43. "Hassan," *The Adelphi* I (December, 1923), 619 - 20.

44. "The Golden Journey," *Saturday Review* CXXXVI (September 29, 1923), 349 - 50.

45. Allardyce Nicoll, *British Drama*, 4th ed. (London: Harrap, 1955), p. 402.

46. G. Wilson Knight, *The Golden Labyrinth* (London, 1962), p. 337.

47. *Ibid.*, p. 3.

48. *Letters to Frank Savery*, p. 98.

49. *Hassan*, pp. 110 - 11.

50. *Ibid.*, pp. 164 - 65.

51. *Ibid.*, pp. 86 - 87.

52. *Ibid.*, pp. 85 - 86. It is interesting to note that W. B. Yeats strongly disapproved of Flecker's portrayal of Haroun-al-Raschid (as he did of *Hassan* in general), declaring that Flecker had completely misrepresented the man. Flecker's representation, he wrote, is disgusting, and made him see in the play "nothing but the perversity and petulance of the disease from which its author was already fading." He continued: "We know Harun al-Rashid through the *Arabian Nights* alone, and there he is the greatest of all

traditional images of generosity and magnanimity. In one beautiful story he finds that a young girl of his harem loves a certain young man, and though he himself loves the girl he sets her free and arranges her marriage; and there are other stories of like import. . . ." (From "On the Boiler," reprinted in *Explorations* [London: 1965], pp. 447 - 49).

53. *Hassan*, p. 139.
54. *Ibid.*, pp. 169 - 70.
55. *Ibid.*, p. 171.
56. *Ibid.*, pp. 182 - 83.
57. It is said by those now living in Areiya who are able to remember Flecker's short stay there that the Fleckers were always quarrelling (See "James Elroy Flecker," *An-Nahar*, January 14, 1968, pp. 16 - 17). Also, T. E. Lawrence's portrait of Hellé Flecker suggests that, though she was gracious and ladylike, she needed all her resources to cope with her self-assertive, somewhat neurotic husband:

Mrs. Flecker, the poised dignity and sweetness of her. The pure correction to what was garish and excessive in Flecker, super-abundant. May one call him a little Jewish in his love of colour and scent, his rioting task. Downright English in his physical brutality and efficiency, his fighting fists, his long springy stride which carried him through the knee-deep asphodel, up and down the rock-slopes of Lebanon, behind Beyrout, his classical bent thrilled to discover traces of Imperial Rome here in a rock-cut road, there in an inscription, or in the lovely aqueduct which spanned Beyrout river just above the town.

Flecker was a Gadarene Greek, and kinsman of Maleager whose poems he came too near worshipping to hope to translate — spendthrift of emotion, loving men and sometimes women, showy, joyous (sulking when ill soon to despair), feeling every joy and sorrow sharply, always embroidering, curling, powdering, painting, his loves and his ideals, demonstrative, showy, self-advertising happy. (Lawrence, p. 4)

58. Knight, p. 337.
59. Priscilla Thouless, *Modern Poetic Drama* (Oxford, 1934), pp. 32 - 34.

Chapter Six

1. *Collected Poems*, pp. 54 - 55.
2. Frank Kermode, *Romantic Image* (London: Routledge-Kegan Paul, 1957), p. 87. It has also been suggested — though less plausibly — that Flecker's Pervaneh in *Hassan* influenced G. B. Shaw's St. Joan in the play of that name. (Herbert Palmer, *Post Victorian Poetry*. [London, 1938], p. 156.)
3. Palmer, p. 146.
4. *Collected Prose*, p. 240.
5. In Robert H. Ross's book on the Georgian movement, *The Georgian Revolt: Rise and Fall of a Poetic Ideal*, Flecker's name is hardly mentioned at all, and then only in terms of his contributions to the Georgian anthologies.

6. *Some Letters From Abroad*, p. 145. It is interesting to note, however, that in a lecture at Cambridge on "the contemporary poet," Monro referred to Flecker as an "impressionist," mentioning him in the same breath as Pound. (Hassall, *Rupert Brooke*, p. 365.)

7. *Ibid.*, p. 146.

8. *Collected Poems*, p. 216. Cf. Richard Middleton. *Poems and Songs*, (London: T. Fisher Unwin, 1912), p. 37.

9. Hassall, *Edward Marsh*, p. 196.

10. Even Flecker's detractors were obliged to admit that as a poetic craftsman there were few among his contemporaries who were his equal. Edward Thomas, for example, writing to W. H. Hudson commented: "[James Elroy Flecker] is one of the 'artificers in verse' that I can't quite get on with, the decorators, like Wilde, who carry Keats' style to its logical extreme without genius. But he did it very well indeed. There are passages reminding me of some of the solid French rhetoricians in verse like Lecompte de Lisle [*sic*]. And if you want brass or even gold why not have it in metal? Words can't be given that character without losing their own, it seems to me." (John Moore, *The Life and Letters of Edward Thomas* [London: Heinemann, 1939], p. 331.)

11. Robert Lynd, *Old and New Masters* (London, 1919), pp. 112 - 13.

12. *Collected Poems*, p. 216.

Selected Bibliography

PRIMARY SOURCES

1. Flecker's main published works are as follows:
The Bridge of Fire. London: Elkin Mathews, 1907.
Thirty-Six Poems. London: Adelphi Press, 1910.
The Grecians. London: J. M. Dent, 1910.
The Scholars' Italian Book. London: David Nutt, 1911.
Forty-Two Poems. London: J. M. Dent, 1911.
The Golden Journey to Samarkand. London: Max Goschen, 1913.
The King of Alsander. London: Max Goschen, 1914.
The Old Ships. London: The Poetry Bookshop, 1915.
Hassan. London: Heinemann, 1922.
Don Juan. London: Heinemann, 1925.
Hassan (an acting edition). London: Heinemann, 1951.
As Flecker was in the habit of continually revising his poetry, the definitive edition of his verse must be the *Collected Poems*, edited and introduced by J. C. Squire, 3rd edition, London: Martin Secker, 1946. This may be supplemented by *James Elroy Flecker: Unpublished Poems and Drafts*, which contains two uncollected poems, "Propertius 1, 20 Hylas" (*sic*) and "[Untitled]," and also "A Prayer to the Brightness of Day" and "For Christians 1912," the last two being revised and published as "Hexameters" and "A Sacred Dialogue," respectively. (The first edition of the *Collected Poems* [1916] is not complete, and though the second edition of 1935 contains twenty additional poems, there are also innumerable misprints, not corrected until the third edition in 1946.) The most accessible volume of his shorter prose pieces is the *Collected Prose*, London: G. Bell, 1920, or the second issue, published by Heinemann in 1922.
2. Correspondence
Most of Flecker's correspondence has also been published, much of it containing critical observations of his own work and that of others, as well as short descriptive sketches of many of the places he visited. The two published volumes of his correspondence are:

The Letters of J. E. Flecker to Frank Savery. London: The Beaumont Press,
    1926.
*Some Letters From Abroad of James Elroy Flecker, With a Few
    Reminiscences by Hellé Flecker and an Introduction by J. C. Squire.*
    London: Heinemann, 1930. (Contains many but not all of Flecker's
    letters to Frank Savery included in the earlier volume.)

SECONDARY SOURCES

1. Biographies, Criticism

HODGSON, GERALDINE. *James Elroy Flecker, From Letters and Materials
    Provided by His Mother.* Oxford: Basil Blackwell, 1925. Until very
    recently this was the only authoritative critical biography of Flecker
    available. Its subtitle indicates its limitations, being a rather too
    favorable account of the man and his work.
SHERWOOD, JOHN. *No Golden Journey: A Biography of James Elroy Flecker.*
    London: Heinemann, 1973. Written by Flecker's nephew on the basis
    of a wealth of family papers, this biography not only supplements
    Geraldine Hodgson's work, but also corrects several misconceptions
    about Flecker which resulted from her too partial account. In par-
    ticular Sherwood reveals that Flecker's relationship with his parents
    was somewhat uneasy, and also points to his strong streak of sado-
    masochism.
GILLANDER, RONALD A. "A Critical Study of James Elroy Flecker." Ph. D.
    dissertation, University of London, 1954. By far the most useful and
    comprehensive account of Flecker's work, this exhaustive study — it
    has 647 pages plus a bibliography — lacks critical focus, and Flecker's
    personality and actual literary achievement tend to be submerged un-
    der mountains of detail; but it remains the fullest, most informative
    account that has so far appeared.
GOLDRING, DOUGLAS. *James Elroy Flecker.* London: Chapman and Hall,
    1922. An appreciative but not especially incisive account of Flecker's
    work, and some reminiscences. Rather more objective than Hodgson,
    however. Contains a descriptive bibliography of Flecker's principal
    published writings.
LAWRENCE, T. E. *An Essay on Flecker.* London: Corvinus Press, 1937. This
    excellent, brief essay, reprinted with slight changes in Lawrence's
    Men In Print (London: Golden Cockerel Press, 1940), is a critical
    assessment of Flecker's personality as it struck the author during a
    brief stay with the Fleckers in Lebanon.
MERCER, T. STANLEY. *James Elroy Flecker: From School to Samarkand.*
    Thames Ditton, Surrey: The Merle Press, 1952. Short rambling ac-
    count of Flecker's school years at Dean Close, which reminds one of
    the antagonism of Flecker's parents to their son's literary achieve-
    ments. Contains a good descriptive bibliography of Flecker's writings,
    more complete than Goldring's.

2. Selected essays, articles, reviews, and books containing references to Flecker and his work

BLOCK, EDWARD ARNOLD. "Rupert Brooke and Flecker." *Poetry Review* X (1929): 23 - 35. Sympathetic, comparative study of the two poets which emphasizes their imitative virtuosity.

BLUEN, HERBERT. "Poet of the Sun." *The Aryan Path* XXXI, 3 (March, 1960): 110 - 14. Rather superficial view of Flecker's achievement; suggests that the fascination of his poetry lies in its orientalism.

BRONNER, M. "James Elroy Flecker: English Parnassian." *Bookman* XLIII (August, 1916): 631 - 36. Appreciative account of Flecker's achievement; stresses his relationship with the Parnassian movement.

BULLARD, SIR READER. "James Elroy Flecker in Constantinople." *The Listener*, February 15, 1951, pp. 268 - 69. Personal reminiscence by a member of the foreign service who knew Flecker in Constantinople.

BYNG, L. CRAMMER. "Flecker's *Hassan*." *Poetry Review* XIV (January, 1923): 33 - 35. Insists that Flecker's play should be judged under the dramatist's own terms: i.e., whether or not he has succeeded in "creating beauty".

GOWDA, H. H. ANNIAH. *The Revival of English Poetic Drama.* Bangaloore, India: Government Press, 1963. Contains a section on Flecker's drama seen in relation to such early twentieth-century verse dramatists as Symons, Davidson, Laurence Binyon, and Gordon Bottomley.

HASSALL, CHRISTOPHER. *Rupert Brooke.* London: Longman's, 1964. Especially useful as an account of Cambridge during Flecker's stay there, when he was friendly with Rupert Brooke.

———. *Edward Marsh: Patron of the Arts.* London: Longman's, 1959. Reveals how much Flecker was indebted to Marsh for the publication of *Hassan*.

"James Elroy Flecker." *An-Nahar*, January 14, 1968, pp. 16 - 17. A short account in Arabic of Flecker's stay in Lebanon, with some personal reminiscences by Mrs. Farida Al-Akl who, besides knowing Flecker, taught T. E. Lawrence Arabic.

KNIGHT, GEORGE WILSON. *The Golden Labyrinth.* London: Phoenix House, 1962. Contains appreciative account of Flecker's achievement as a dramatist; draws attention to *Hassan* as one of the best dramas of the early twentieth century.

LESLIE, SHANE. *The Cantab.* London: Chatto and Windus, 1926. A novel which reflects undergraduate life at Cambridge in Flecker's day; valuable for thinly disguised portraits of such people as Baron Corvo and Oscar Browning, who may have exerted some influence on Flecker's development.

LYND, ROBERT. *Old and New Masters.* London: T. Fisher Unwin, 1919. Contains a sensible but brief chapter on Flecker's achievement as a writer.

MACDONALD, ALEC. "James Elroy Flecker." *Fortnightly Review* CXV (February, 1924): 274 - 84. Sympathetic assessment of Flecker's achievement by one who believes that "the death of Flecker at the age of thirty-one is unquestionably the greatest premature loss that English literature has suffered since the death of Keats."

MACKENZIE, COMPTON. *Sinister Street.* 2 vols. London: Martin Secker, 1912 - 14. A four-part novel of which section three, "Dreaming Spires," is an account of Oxford while Flecker was there.

MASON, EUGENE. *Considered Writers: Old and New.* London: Methuen, 1925, pp. 27 - 48. Sympathetic account of Flecker's achievement, stresses the Symbolist and Oriental influences on his poetry.

MEGROZ, R. L. *Modern English Poetry.* London: Nicholson Watson, 1933. Contains sympathetic account of Flecker as a poet; draws attention to some of the influences on his work.

MURRY, JOHN MIDDLETON. "Hassan." *The Adelphi* I (December, 1923): 619 - 20. A review of *Hassan*; emphasizes its qualities as a spectacle; but expresses reservations about its literary worth.

PALMER, HERBERT. *Post Victorian Poetry.* London: Dent, 1938. Contains a chapter on Flecker which stresses his role in the Georgian movement; a highly appreciative assessment.

ROUTH, H. V. *English Literature and Ideas in the Twentieth Century.* London: Methuen, 1946. A somewhat negative assessment; emphasizes that Flecker knew much about art but little about life.

"TARN." "Hassan, by James Elroy Flecker." *Spectator* CXXXI (September 29, 1923): 418 - 19. Appreciative review of Flecker's play.

Times Literary Supplement, September 28, 1916, pp. 457 - 58. A leading article on Flecker; one of the soundest critical assessments Flecker has received.

THOULESS, PRISCILLA. *Modern Poetic Drama.* Oxford: Blackwell's, 1935. Probably the best assessment of Flecker as a dramatist; his status is reviewed in relation to other verse dramatists of the twentieth century.

WOLFE, HUMBERT. "James Elroy Flecker and the Red Man." In *Portraits by Inference.* London: Methuen, 1934. Rather snide account of Flecker as he appeared as a young man; stresses his wit and high spirits.

Index